Give Me a Home Where the Dairy Cows Roam

Give Me a Home Where the Dairy Cows Roam

(True Stories from a Wisconsin Farm)

LeAnn R. Ralph

~ Dedication ~

In memory of my father:
Roy Arthur Ralph (1914 - 1992)
And my mother:
Norma Irene Halvorson Ralph (1916 - 1985)

And for the dairy farmers of Wisconsin—and all farmers everywhere.

A friend of mine says, "If you ate something today, thank a farmer!"

I'd like to take that a step farther.

"If you drink milk or eat cheese, cottage cheese, yogurt, butter, whipped cream, or put cream in your coffee—thank a dairy farmer!"

****

~ About the Cover ~

The cow on the right was a Guernsey in our dairy herd named Number. If you look closely at the bottom of her neck, you can see my twine string reins.

Number appears in the first story, "Back in the Saddle Again." She was part of our dairy herd more years ago than I care to count, and I like to think she received some sort of reward for being so kind to a pesky kid who always wanted a horse—that somewhere in the Great Beyond, she grazes in an everlasting pasture, up to her knees in clover and alfalfa.

****

~ Foreword ~

Forty years ago when I was growing up on our dairy farm in Wisconsin, I would walk around the buildings yelling for my father. I'd wait for an answering "Hi!" and then I would go in that direction.

Dad (who was forty-four when I was born) usually was doing something interesting. One time when I was about four or five, I helped him grease the hay baler.

Well, all right, what *really* happened is that Dad didn't notice I had gotten into the grease until it was much too late. I ended up with gobs of the dark purple stuff all over myself, from my hands up to my elbows, on my clothes and on my face.

Another time, the sound of a hammer attracted me to the machine shed where I found Dad in the middle of building a hay rack. He drew lines where he wanted the nails to go, made sure I knew how to drive a nail in straight, and then he gave me the hammer.

I went to work pounding nails.

When we were finished building the rack, Dad let me help paint it too. A nice bright red. Then, while the paint was wet, we threw sand on it. "That will help keep it from being so slippery when we bale hay," Dad had explained.

I helped my father with many tasks around the farm. Cows in labor sometimes needed a little assistance, so Dad showed me how to apply gentle tension on a rope tied to the calf's front feet. After a while, there would be the calf, all wet and shaking its head.

As I grew older still, Dad taught me how to drive a tractor and how to load a hay wagon, how to change oil and how to turn a wrench.

I lived away from my hometown for fifteen years. I worked on a thoroughbred farm in Kentucky and a Tennessee walking horse farm in the southern part of Wisconsin. I earned a bachelor's degree and a master's degree in English. I wrote for a newspaper. I taught English at a boys' boarding school.

Eleven years after my mother died and two years after Dad passed away, my husband and I moved back to west central Wisconsin to live in the house my parents had built when they retired from farming.

Before I returned to my hometown, I fully expected to be living in a farming community again.

Instead, I discovered that while I was gone, many of the small family dairy farms had disappeared, farms like the one where I grew up when my dad milked twenty cows and knew each of them by name.

According to statistics from the United States Census of Agriculture, during the last three decades of the twentieth century, Wisconsin lost two-thirds of its dairy farms. In 1969—when I was 11 years old—there were 66,000 dairy farms in the state. In 1980, there were 44,000. By the year 2000, the number had fallen to 22,000.

Nationwide statistics show the same trend.

Figures from the Census of Agriculture and from the American Farm Bureau Federation indicate that since 1969, the United States has lost 85 percent of its dairy farms. In 1969, more than a half million dairy farms operated in the United States, but by 1988, less than a quarter of a million remained. (Census of Agriculture). And by the year 2000, the numbers had fallen farther yet to only 83,000 dairy farms (American Farm Bureau Federation).

So, considering the circumstances, if I happen to drive down a country road and spy a herd of dairy cattle turned out to pasture, I feel like I should stop and take a picture.

A few times, too, I have rounded a curve or topped a hill, and was surprised to find houses and garages where there used to be pastures, cornfields and hayfields.

Then there's the feed mill in my hometown. Not so long ago, a half-dozen pickup trucks would be waiting to have their loads of corn and oats ground into feed for dairy cattle.

In 2003, the fire department burned the feed mill to the ground as a training exercise for firefighters. A parking lot now occupies the space where I used to spend summer afternoons with my dad while we waited for our corn and oats to be made into feed for the dairy cows.

LeAnn R. Ralph
Colfax, Wisconsin

****

~ 1 ~
Back in the Saddle Again

I knew if I could only stretch another inch or two, my fingers would reach their goal. I stood on tiptoes, drew a deep breath and pushed my arm down into the fifty-five gallon drum. My hand closed on thin air.

"What're you doing?"

I whirled around. "Oh, Daddy! You scared me."

My father set down the full milker bucket, and the group of barn cats that had been following him clustered around their dish a few feet away, meowing and watching him expectantly. From the platform above the twine barrel came the steady hum of the milker pump, and from farther along the barn aisle, the swish-swish of the vacuum lines meant the milking machines were hard at work.

I looked up into my father's sky-blue eyes. "I need some twine string but I can't quite reach it."

"What do you need twine string for?" he asked and then held up one calloused hand. "No, don't tell me. I bet you're chasing bank robbers tonight. Or maybe it's a run-away stage coach this time?"

He reached far into the barrel and pulled out a fistful of strings. "Here. Take what you want and put the rest back."

My father picked up the bucket and poured some milk into the cat dish, turned toward the door and paused with his hand on the handle.

"Just remember that not all the cows are as friendly as Number," he cautioned.

"I know, Dad."

And with that, he disappeared into the darkness, headed toward the milkhouse to dump the bucket.

From the time I was a very little girl—small enough to be wearing a pink, one-piece snowsuit with a pointed hood—I liked to be out in the barn with Dad at milking time. And early on, I had learned there were two kinds of dairy cows in our barn, nice ones and mean ones. The nice cows were reddish brown (Guernseys). The mean cows were black and white (Holsteins).

The nice cows didn't mind when I ran up and down the barn aisles, shrieking and laughing. They would watch me for a few seconds, and then they would go back to calmly eating their hay.

The mean cows, on the other hand, got a wild look in their eyes, shook their heads threateningly, lashed their tails and sometimes even let loose with the lightning-fast kick of a hind foot.

I asked my father once why we didn't have all Guernseys instead of Guernseys and Holsteins. Dad said he kept a few Guernseys in the herd because their milk had more butterfat and that a higher percentage of butterfat meant he received a better price for the milk. We had Holsteins, he said, because they gave more milk than Guernseys, even though it wasn't as rich as Guernsey milk.

As I stood there selecting which twine strings I wanted, a chilly breeze blew into the barn from Dad opening and closing the door. It was still cold outside even though it was early spring.

'These should work all right," I said, choosing twine strings that had been cut, rather than strings that were all in one piece.

Sometimes when my father opened a bale of hay, he pulled the strings off so they were still held together by the knot the baler had tied. Most of the time, however, he used his pocket knife to cut the strings. The twine I held in my hands gave off a sharp, almost bitter odor, but it was a good smell, too, because it reminded me of alfalfa and clover blossoms and long summer days with clear blue skies.

I tossed the rest of the twine string into the barrel and headed toward the other end of the barn to find the Guernsey cow we called Number. Dad had bought her at an auction, and when he brought her home, she was wearing the number sixteen. That's why we called her Number.

In our barn, the cows were lined up side by side in adjoining stalls with their heads facing the outer wall and their tails facing a center aisle. Dad said some barns were the opposite way, with the cows facing the center aisle and their tails toward the wall, but I had never been in a barn like that.

My father had already finished milking on the far end of the barn, so some of the cows were taking a nap, their legs folded under them in their golden beds of straw. Others stood, either eating hay with a thoughtful expression on their faces, or were chewing their cuds, jaws moving sideways to grind their food.

I walked a few more steps, and there she was. "Hi, Number," I said.

The Guernsey cow turned her head to look at me. Number was the prettiest cow I had ever seen. Her deep-red color stood out among her black and white neighbors, and she had a funny little white mark in the center of her 'mooly' forehead. Once in a while a calf will be born without horns. Even on a newborn, you can feel the bumps on the top of their heads that will someday turn into horns, but the mooly calves didn't have any horns at all and never would. Just like Number.

"We're going for a ride," I said. "Okay?"

Still watching me with a gentle expression in her dark-brown eyes, the cow continued chewing her cud.

I stepped across the gutter channel.

"I have to fix our reins first," I said, putting my arms around the cow's neck so I could tie the twine string.

Twine, I had discovered, was an extremely useful item. When it wasn't holding bales of hay together, you could use it for all kinds of other things: a dog leash when you're going to the feed mill with your dad, to tie your wagon to the back of your bicycle—or reins when you're going to ride your favorite cow.

As I stood there with my arms around Number's neck, her red hair felt bristly against my cheek, and I could smell her breath, a combination of alfalfa hay and ground feed made out of oats and corn.

"There," I said, when I finished tying the string. "Are you ready?"

As if to answer me, the Guernsey cow swallowed her cud.

I moved back and climbed onto the metal pipe welded to the front of the stall and anchored into the cement floor at the back. Not all of the stalls in the barn had a divider between them, but the one between Number and her neighbor did. As I hoisted myself onto the divider, the Holstein cow next to us jumped sideways, startled by the movement.

From my perch on the stall divider, I scrambled onto Number's back and gathered up my twine string reins. "Giddy-up Number. Let's go!"

More than anything in the world, I wanted a pony, but since I didn't yet have one, Number was the next best thing.

The Guernsey shifted her weight, and a tremor passed through her body that felt like a burp. The tremor signaled she had coughed up another cud so she could continue chewing her food.

"Come on, Number! Giddy-up! The bank robbers are getting away!"

The cow was shut into her stanchion, so she couldn't go anywhere. And she had a sweet-smelling pile of alfalfa hay right in front of her, so where else would she want to go? But that didn't stop me from pretending Number and I were riding the range. I had watched many Westerns on television (as if you couldn't tell), and sometimes I imagined we were going to town. Or that we were checking fences. Occasionally we tried to stop a runaway stage coach.

This time we were part of a posse, and in a short while the excitement of the moment caught up with me again.

"Yeehaaa!!!" I shouted.

Number shifted her weight, and all the while, her jaws moved up and down and around, chewing her cud.

"Yeeeeehaaaaaa!!!" I shouted again.

At the sound of my second "yeehaa!!" Number's neighbor jumped sideways and pulled back in her stanchion. The whites of her eyes showed, and as her tail swished, I wondered if she could hit Number if she decided to kick. I didn't want my friend to get kicked. I had never been kicked myself, but according to Dad and my big brother, Ingman, it wasn't much fun.

"All right," Dad called from the other end of the barn. "That's enough. Don't make so much noise, or else go outside. You're scaring the cows."

I looked around, and all up and down the barn, black and white Holsteins were staring in our direction.

"Sorry, Dad."

If my father said it was time to quit the posse, it was time to quit. I slid off Number's back, untied the twine string, and gave her a final pat on the shoulder. Then I walked to the other end of the barn and put my reins back into the twine barrel, an empty fifty-five gallon drum

Ingman had brought home from his job at the creamery in town six miles away.

Sometimes my friends at school asked me about my brother's name. Ingman is named for our Norwegian grandmother, Inga, and he is twenty-one years older than me. My sister, Loretta, is nineteen years older. When Ingman and Loretta were three and five, Mom, who was twenty-six at the time, had been stricken with polio and paralyzed in both legs. After the polio, the doctors told her she would never have more children. I was born sixteen years later when Mom was forty-two and Dad was forty-four.

As I replaced the cover on the twine barrel, Dad picked up another full milker bucket.

"Have fun?" he asked, once again stopping by the cat dish. He nudged aside a couple of cats so he could move closer, and then he tipped a little of the warm milk into the dish. When he left the barn, I followed behind him into the frosty night air.

"Daddy?" I began, as he stepped into the milkhouse.

"Huh?" he said, lifting the heavy milker bucket to dump it into the strainer. A filter in the bottom of the strainer caught any stray cow hairs that might have gotten into the bucket. The milk ran through the strainer and into a milk can, and when the can was full, Dad would put the cover on it and set it in the cooling tank next to the other cans. The tank was built of concrete and filled with water to help cool the milk.

"Dad, why won't the other cows let me ride them?" I asked.

"Hmmmm," he said, tipping the bucket almost on end so all of the milk would pour out. "Maybe they don't think they should be horses."

"But why not? Number is my horse."

"Number is different."

"How come?" I asked.

"She's a Guernsey, and she loves little girls who sit on her back and pretend they're chasing bank robbers," Dad explained.

"How do you know?"

Dad winked. "She told me so."

"Daddy! She did not. Cows can't talk!"

"Maybe not with words, but they can still let you know what they think."

I followed him back to the barn, considering what he had said.

"How can you tell what cows are thinking?" I asked, looking at the Holstein Dad was going to milk next.

The cow moved over as he stepped up by her. When he started to wash her udder, she lifted one hind foot and then set it down gingerly.

"This one," Dad said, as he continued washing with a cloth soaked in warm water and iodine soap, "is thinking that I shouldn't scrub so hard."

"Can you tell what the kitties are thinking, too?" I asked, as a cat rubbed its head against my ankle. Other cats were grooming, although one old tabby sat quietly, tail curled around her front paws, watching Dad's every movement.

"That one by your feet is thinking she'd like you to pick her up and pet her. Our old momma kitty, there, is thinking I ought to hurry up and dump more milk in their dish," he replied.

I picked up the cat who was winding herself around my ankles, and she snuggled down in my arms.

"But how you do know what Number is thinking?" I asked.

"I just know," Dad said. "If she didn't like the attention, she wouldn't stand so quiet."

Letting me sit on her back while she chewed her cud wasn't all that I required of Number, however. Certainly not.

As the spring days became warmer, I waited for the grass to grow long enough so the cows could be turned out to pasture, and then when Dad or Ingman went out to bring the cows to the barn for milking, I went with them—taking a set of twine string reins with me, of course.

The trip back to the barn was always glorious. Instead of pretending the Guernsey and I were riding the range, we actually were.

Well, sort of, anyway.

Our farm was only one-hundred-and-twenty acres so there wasn't much of a 'range.' But there was a lovely dirt lane next to the big wooded hill behind the barn that we called the Bluff—and that was good enough for me.

****

~ 2 ~
Taking the Bull by the Horns

D ad finished tying his brown leather work boots and then stood up to reach for his coat. "What time do you think you'll be home?" my mother asked as I carried the first stack of dinner dishes to the sink.

For Sunday dinner we'd had pot roast with potatoes and gravy and carrots and onions, which is what we usually ate for Sunday dinner.

A little more than a week ago, the last of the snow had melted, and although the lawn was brown, a few hints of green gave me hope that soon it would be warm enough so I wouldn't have to wear a coat when I went to school. I could hardly wait for the weather to be warm enough so I didn't have to wear a coat.

Dad must have been thinking about warmer weather too, because while we were eating dinner, he had announced that he wanted to go sucker fishing. On Sunday afternoons in early spring right after the snow had melted and the ground was still wet and the grass was still brown, Dad often went sucker fishing.

The fish were full of bones and not very good to eat, unless they were pickled, but after the weather warmed up and the ground dried out, my father would begin plowing so he could plant oats. And once he started the field work, Dad wouldn't have time to go fishing.

My father zipped up his lined denim chore coat and settled a blue-and-white-pin-striped cap onto his head. Even when Dad went to the grocery store or to the drug store on an errand for my mother, who had never learned to drive and couldn't learn how to drive now because of the polio paralysis, he wore a blue-and-white pin-striped cap. The only difference was that when he went to town, he wore a brand new cap he kept especially for that purpose.

"What time will I be home?" Dad said, as he turned to look at the old butter-yellow Time-A-Trol clock the electric company had installed next to the kitchen sink many years ago. "We won't be gone *that* long. Only a couple of hours. It's kind of chilly today," he said.

If anyone had asked me, I would have pointed out that it was not 'kind of chilly.' It was downright cold. The sky was cloudy, and a raw, damp wind blew out of the south. Dad said the south wind meant that in a day or two, the weather would turn warmer.

My father opened the door leading into the porch. "I'll be back after a while," he said and closed the door behind him.

When Dad said "we won't be gone that long," unfortunately, the 'we' did not include 'me.' Dad was going fishing with my mother's cousin, Garfield. The two cousins, Garfield and Reuben, had grown up not far from our farm. They were the sons of my grandfather's brother, and they thought of my mother more like a younger sister rather than a cousin. My mother was an only child. Both of her parents were immigrants from Norway, and when Mom was a little girl, they spoke only Norwegian at home. My great-grandfather homesteaded our farm in the late 1800s, and Mom had lived here her whole life.

Sometimes if Dad and Garfield went fishing on a Sunday afternoon during the summer, they would take me with them. But Dad wouldn't let me go sucker fishing because at this time of year, the water was high from melted snow. And since Dad claimed he didn't feel as young as he used to and that he didn't like the idea of fishing for his youngest daughter if she fell in the river, for the time being, I had to be content with helping Mom and Loretta do the dinner dishes. While my mother washed, Loretta and I dried the dishes and put them away.

After the dishes were finished, I wasn't quite sure what to do with myself. It wasn't warm enough outside to ride my bike, and we didn't have any neighbors with children for me to play with.

"Why don't you read a book?" Mom suggested as she settled into her chair by the picture window in the living room. Mom spent many hours in her chair every day, embroidering pillowcases, dresser scarves and tablecloths she donated to the church to sell at the fall bazaar.

The little white country church a half mile from our farm had been built a long time before I was born. My mother's grandparents, parents, aunts and uncles were part of the church's first congregation. Mom said since she couldn't do much of anything else because of the polio, she might as well make things our church could sell.

As my mother got out her embroidery materials, I looked for a book to read. My favorite books were about horses, and although I had read it many times before, I selected one about the ponies of Chincoteague.

A few minutes later when I sat down in the old wooden rocking chair that had been in the living room for as long as I could remember, I discovered I couldn't concentrate on the words. I kept thinking about Dad and Garfield and about how much fun they were having, fishing for suckers in the river.

After a while, I sighed and closed the book.

"Why don't you play the piano?" suggested Loretta, who was curled up on the davenport with a magazine.

My big sister worked as an assistant bookkeeper for the electric company that supplied electricity to our farm and to many of the rural areas in the county, and on Sunday afternoons, she liked to spend a few hours relaxing. For Loretta, relaxing might mean baking cookies, trying out a new color of fingernail polish, working on a sewing project, or reading one of the women's magazines she subscribed to.

I sat down by the piano and started to play.

A few years ago, I had taken piano lessons from a woman named Lillian. She used to live on the farm next door to ours, but her husband had died unexpectedly, and she had sold the farm and moved to town.

I had learned enough so that I could play the piano with both hands if the songs weren't too complicated. The piano Mom had bought was a heavy, old-fashioned upright. The only music I had were hymns in a book my mother kept in the house for Ladies' Aid meetings. *Rock of Ages*, *Blest Be the Tie that Binds,* and *Silent Night* were my favorites.

After a half an hour, Mom asked me to stop.

"I've got a bit of a headache today. Maybe you could roll some of this embroidery floss into balls. That would be a big help," she said.

I put the music book away and went over to my mother, who gave me a handful of skeins. The embroidery floss came in skeins that were like miniatures of the big skeins of yarn my sister used for knitting.

Rolling skeins of floss into balls was fun. You had to take off the two tiny paper sleeves that held the floss together, fold one of them in half and then roll the floss around the paper. Sometimes it was like a puzzle because the thread would be tangled around itself.

When I was in the middle of the second skein, my mother turned so she could see the kitchen clock. Then she swiveled around to look out the window at the road running south toward the church.

"What's the matter?" I asked.

My mother drew in a deep breath and let it out. "If Dad's gone much longer, he'll be in the barn until midnight," she said.

I glanced at the clock. It was only 3:30.

"It doesn't take that long to milk," I pointed out.

"Maybe not," Mom replied, "but he still has to put the cows in first and feed them."

During the winter, Dad would let the cows out every day so he could clean the barn, although if the temperature was below zero, he wouldn't leave them out for too long because he was afraid they would freeze their udders. But once spring arrived, the cows stayed outside all afternoon. Even though the air felt chilly today, it wasn't cold enough so the cows would freeze their udders, and Dad had said it would be good for them to be outside for a while.

A few minutes later, Mom looked at the clock once again and heaved another deep sigh.

Dad had assured my mother he wouldn't be gone long, but I could tell she was worried about the chores. Mom always worried about the chores, mostly, I think, because she couldn't get around well enough do them herself. When my mother went outside, she walked with crutches, moving one crutch forward and then one foot, one crutch forward and then one foot. Inside the house, she often held onto the furniture and the kitchen counter, rather than using her crutches.

As I rolled another skein of floss, a thought that had been swimming around in the back of my mind suddenly rose to the surface.

"Mom!" I exclaimed. "I just had a great idea."

"An idea?" she said, turning to look at me.

"What if I put the cows in and feed them so Dad won't have to?"

I was in the barn with my father all the time, and I knew exactly what to do. If I put the cows in and fed them, when Dad came home, he wouldn't have to feed the cows first. He could eat supper right away. And not only would it save time for Dad, but Mom could also stop worrying about the chores.

My mother shook her head. "No. I don't want you to put the cows in by yourself."

My anticipation evaporated in the blink of an eye.

"Why not?"

"Because we've got a bull, that's why," she said.

Most of the time, Dad used an artificial insemination service for the cows, but every few years he acquired a bull calf. As the animal grew older, my father would turn the bull loose to run with the herd.

This particular bull was only a yearling, however. And he was friendly. Ever since the Holstein had been a calf, he loved to have his forehead scratched. Of course it was true that over the winter he had grown to be rather large—but he was still my friend.

"Mo-om," I pleaded, "he's just a baby. He won't hurt me. He wouldn't hurt anybody."

"No, I don't want you out there by yourself," she said. "If it was just feeding, that would be one thing. But you'd have to put the cows in."

"Pleeeease? Dad will be soooooooo surprised when he comes home. And I don't get to surprise him very often..."

My sister, who was still sitting on the davenport with her magazine, looked up from the article she was reading.

"What if I go out to help?" Loretta asked.

I felt my eyebrows creeping upward. The only time I saw Loretta come out to the barn was to get a pitcher of milk or to bring some table scraps for our dog, Needles, and the barn cats. When my big sister was on her way to work, or to church, her slim figure dressed in elegant two-piece suits with high heels to match—and sometimes even wearing a hat and gloves—I wondered why she wasn't a model, like the pretty ladies in the magazines, instead of an assistant bookkeeper. Her curly brown hair was never out of place, and she wore pink fingernail polish that matched her lipstick. She smelled good, too, like lilacs or roses.

"Why are you looking at me like that?" Loretta asked. "It's not as if I've never done chores before, you know."

My mouth dropped open in surprise. "You've done chores?"

Loretta tossed down her magazine. "Of *course* I've done chores."

"When?" I asked.

The frown lines smoothed from Loretta's forehead. "Well, I suppose maybe you wouldn't remember. Ingman and I used to do the chores when Dad worked at the canning factory."

"Really?"

"Yes, really. I've milked cows and fed calves and cleaned the barn and baled hay. And yes, I've driven the tractor, too, so don't ask."

"Oh, but Loretta," Mom said, "you don't want to go out in the barn. You'll get so dirty…"

My sister sat up straight. "I will not let her put that bull in by herself," she declared.

"*He is not a bull*," I said, my voice coming out much louder than I intended. "He's just a baby."

"Baby!" Mom exclaimed. "He's already a year old."

Loretta nodded. "That's right. He's hardly a baby."

"Okay, so maybe he's not *technically* a baby, but he's nice. He's my friend."

"Hah!" Mom said. "There's no such thing as a nice bull."

My throat started to tighten up, and I thought maybe I was going to cry. Why couldn't they understand that Bully-loo, as Dad called him, was quite friendly?

"He is too nice," I said, my voice quavering. "If Dad was here, he'd say the same thing."

"All right, all right," Loretta said. "Maybe he is nice. But he's still a bull, and if you're going to put the cows in, I can't let you go out to the barn by yourself."

Now that I had thought about it for a little while, I realized it would be twice as much fun if my sister helped. Besides, then I could show her what I meant about Bully-loo. It didn't seem fair that Mom and Loretta thought Bully-loo was mean just because he was a boy cow.

"You *really* want to help me put the cows in?" I asked.

"It's been years since I've worked in the barn," Loretta said. "It'll be an adventure."

I turned toward Mom. "Pleeeease? If Loretta helps me, pleeeease-pleeeeeeease can I put the cows in?"

My mother blinked once…twice.

"In the first place, it's not 'can I.' You should say 'may I'," she replied. "But—oh—all right. If you're sure you don't mind, Loretta."

"No," she said. "I don't mind. I like the idea of doing something nice for Dad."

A little while later, seeming very much out of place with a colorful scarf tied over her dark hair and one of my brother's chore coats zipped over an old sweatshirt—and wearing an even older pair of pants—my sister helped me measure the cow feed. We put two scoops of the corn and oats mixture into the manger in front of each stanchion.

The cows were milling around in the barnyard, and the occasional "moooooo!" interrupted the clattering of their hooves on the concrete slab in front of the door. The cows knew it was feeding time, and they were more than ready to come inside.

"Are you sure," Loretta asked when we had finished dumping the feed, "that the bull isn't mean?"

"He's nice. You'll see."

"I'll take your word for it, thank you. Do you want me to open the door?"

"No, I can do it," I said.

Just as Dad always did, I opened the door far enough to stick my arm out so I could wave it around. When the cows had moved back, I pushed the door open farther.

One by one, the cows hurried into the barn. I started shutting the stanchions on the north side, and Loretta began shutting stanchions on the south side. Even before I had started going to school, I knew which way was north, south, east and west. The church was south of the farm. The pine trees at the end of the hayfield were west. The road leading to our other place was north. And the neighbor's place was east.

Some of the cows liked to go in the same stall every time but some did not. Dad said cows were like people that way, because some people want the same routine every day while others want a little variety.

Bully-loo, I had noticed, was one of those who liked variety. Sometimes he chose a stall on the north side of the barn, and sometimes he went to the south side.

After I made sure each cow was securely latched into her stanchion, I went to help my sister. I hadn't seen Bully-loo, so I knew he was on the other side of the barn.

"Did everything go all right?" Loretta asked anxiously as I walked along the row of cows toward her. She stood in front of the haymow ladder and leaned forward to latch the last open stanchion.

I stopped beside her. "Why do you want to know if everything went all right?"

"I don't have the bull," Loretta said, "so that must mean you did."

I looked at my sister.

Then I looked at the young black and white bull calmly chewing his feed.

"But that's him right there," I said. "You just shut his stanchion."

With a shriek, my sister turned and was halfway up the haymow ladder in one leap.

I had no idea she could move that fast.

Bully-loo stood there quietly, his jaws going up and down and around as he chewed his feed. When I began to scratch his forehead, the bull's expression grew dreamy, and his raspy tongue darted out to lick my coat.

Loretta slowly climbed down off the ladder, never taking her eyes from Bully-loo.

"Want to pet him?" I asked, as Bully began licking my pants. I looked down and saw he had smeared soggy cow feed all over my coat and that he was getting it on my jeans, too.

"Bully-loo," I said in my sternest voice, tapping him on the nose, "stop that."

Bully waggled his ears—and then went back to licking my pants.

I glanced at Loretta. "Come and pet him."

Wide-eyed, my sister backed farther away and shook her head.

"No, no. That's all right," she said.

"You *like* being petted, don't you Bully-loo," I said, scratching around his ears. "See?"

Loretta stopped retreating.

"Just pet him a little bit. Please? He won't hurt you."

"Oh," Loretta said, sounding resigned, "all right. Just a little."

As my sister approached, Bully-loo stopped licking my jeans and turned his gaze toward her.

"Why is he looking at me like that?" she asked.

"What do you mean, 'like that?' How's he supposed to look?"

While Loretta was still several feet away, she leaned forward, extended one finger, and tickled the middle of Bully's broad forehead. Once again, his eyes grew dreamy and the raspy tongue went back to licking my coat.

Loretta laughed and came closer. Bully-loo abruptly leaned forward. The wood and metal stanchion groaned under his weight, and in fact, up and down the line, the metal creaked from the pressure.

"*Now* what's he doing?" Loretta asked, sounding nervous again.

I looked at Bully-loo. "I think he wants to lick your coat."

Loretta's eyes widened. She lifted one hand to tug the scarf down over her ears more securely. "Oh, err, I...I... don't know, I—"

Just then I heard the barn door open.

"Hey!" Dad said. "Who put the cows in?"

"We did," I answered.

Moments later, he was striding toward us. "They're all in? And the stanchions are all shut? And they've got plenty of feed?"

"Yes, Daddy."

"Well...and there's Bully-loo," he said, stopping to scratch the bull's forehead. He looked at Loretta. "Been petting Bully?"

My sister drew a deep, shaky breath and then let it out. "A little," she replied.

Dad smiled. "Did he lick your coat?"

Loretta shook her head. "I haven't dared get that close."

My father patted the bull's muscular neck. "We got lucky this time. Bully-loo's friendly."

Loretta moved a few steps closer. She reached out, hesitated, and then began scratching around the base of Bully's ears.

Once again, Bully-loo's eyes softened. He turned his head and began licking Loretta's coat.

"Mom and Loretta didn't want me to put the cows in because they said Bully-loo was mean just because he's a bull. I told them and told them that Bully was nice, but they wouldn't believe me," I said.

Dad patted Bully-loo's neck again. "Yup, he's a nice boy, all right." He turned his head toward me. "But don't ever forget that he *is* a bull and that you might not always be able to trust him."

My sister threw a meaningful glance in my direction.

"But," I said, staring at Dad in astonishment, "Bully is our friend!"

Dad put his arm around the bull's neck. "Yes, Bully-loo is our friend. And I think he's going to continue to be our friend. But always remember that he is a very large friend."

All at once, Bully-loo must have remembered he hadn't finished his feed because he went back to eating it.

"Bully's got the right idea," Dad said. "I think it's time for supper too."

We still had to give the cows hay, and while Dad threw bales down from the mow, Loretta and I cut them open. In a little while Dad joined us, and with three of us feeding hay, the job went quickly.

"Did you catch any fish?" Loretta asked as we walked side by side toward the barn door on our way back to the house for supper.

Dad shook his head. "Nope. Not a one. Must not have moved into the river yet."

"Oh, Daddy," I said. "You hardly ever get to go fishing but then you didn't catch anything."

My father turned to me. "That's okay. If I hadn't gone fishing, then I wouldn't have seen what I did."

"What did you see?" Loretta asked, a puzzled look in her pretty blue eyes.

Dad winked. "My two girls—taking the bull by the horns—so to speak. Even though Bully-loo doesn't have any." He shook his head. "No, I never would have believed it if I hadn't seen it with my own eyes. Imagine that, your sister letting a bull lick her coat."

"I was right there, and I *still* don't believe it," Loretta said.

I looked over at my big sister.

To tell you the truth—I sort of had trouble believing it myself.

****

~ 3 ~
Spring Cleaning

W hen I reached the top of the driveway after getting off the school bus one April afternoon, I couldn't help but wonder why Dad was standing on the stepladder next to the tractor. I had never seen my father use a stepladder to fix a tractor. He didn't have to climb on anything to reach the engine. I also knew he wasn't filling the tractor with gasoline. The 460 Farmall was too far away from the gas barrel underneath the silver maple tree by the garage, so the hose wouldn't reach that far.

"What's Dad doing Needles?" I asked.

Our dog, Needles, had come to meet me, his tail going in circles. Needles was a Cocker Spaniel-Spitz mix we had gotten when he was a tiny cream-colored puppy with wavy hair on his ears. Within the first week, he had nipped my sister's ankles while she was hanging clothes outside to dry. She had exclaimed, "Get those needles out of here!" And the name had stuck. As Needles grew older, his color had darkened to light caramel.

At the sound of the word, 'Dad,' Needles' ears perked up, and his round brown eyes stared at me with sharpened intensity. Needles was Dad's 'hired man.' That's what Dad said, anyway. When my father worked in the field, the dog would either trot behind the tractor or, on warmer days, would find some shade at the end of the field where he could keep an eye on things.

"What's Dad doing?" I repeated. "Go find Dad, Needles."

The dog, his feathery tail still wagging, spun around and took off toward the machine shed.

I stood for a minute, listening to the redwing blackbirds singing in the marsh below our driveway—on-ka-leeee-eeeeee…on-ka-leeeee-eeeeee. From the pasture next to the barn, meadowlarks joined in—tweedle-ee-tweedle-eedle-um…tweedle-ee-tweedle-eedle-um.

As I turned toward the house, my books tucked in the crook of one arm and my jacket draped over the other, I still couldn't quite believe the sun was shining. For the past two weeks, the weather had been cold and rainy, but today the dark clouds had gone away and the sun had appeared. During afternoon recess at school, it was so warm we had all taken off our jackets.

Last night at supper, Dad said he wished it would stop raining, and I knew this was the kind of weather he had been waiting for so he could plant oats and corn. He wouldn't start for a few days, though, not until he was sure the fields were dried out and that he wouldn't get stuck in the mud with the tractor.

Although I usually went into the house right away when I arrived home from school, today I set my books on the porch steps. For some reason, now that the snow had melted and the grass had turned green, the house looked bigger. My mother said our house was nothing more than a glorified log cabin, and underneath the white slate siding it *was* a log cabin built by my Norwegian great-grandfather.

The rumbling in my stomach reminded me it had been a long time since lunch. I liked to eat a snack as soon as I came home from school, but with Dad working outside by the machine shed, curiosity got the better of me, and I figured I could always eat a snack later.

As I approached the machine shed, I could see a green bottle standing on the engine cowling next to Dad's elbow and a wad of rags hanging out of his back pocket. Dad was wearing faded blue work overalls and a blue short-sleeved chambray shirt. During the winter, he wore long-sleeved plaid flannel shirts, but during the summer, he wore short-sleeved shirts.

"What're you doing?" I asked.

My father looked up quickly, as if he were surprised someone had spoken to him. Needles sat beside the tractor, keeping a watchful eye on Dad.

"Home from school so soon?" Dad asked, reaching for his pocket watch. "Well, yes, I guess it is that time already, isn't it."

I had asked him once why he carried a pocket watch. He said a wrist watch would get too dirty from the dust, oil and grease and would probably stop working. All of his work overalls had a watch pocket, a small slit above the regular pocket. A black leather watch fob threaded through one of his front belt loops kept the watch from falling on the ground if it accidentally came out of his pocket.

The four-sixty had been around for almost as long as I could remember. It had been brand new when Dad bought it. The tractor had bright red fenders and alternating red and white sections above the engine. The rear tires, as black as licorice, were much taller than me.

Dad called the four-sixty 'the big tractor,' and he called the Super C Farmall 'the little tractor.' He used the four-sixty for all of the heavy field work: plowing and planting in the spring, cutting and baling hay during the summer, harvesting oats in August—right around the time of my birthday or maybe a little later—and for picking corn in the fall.

Sometimes when Dad went to our 'other place,' a second farm my parents owned a mile away, he would let me ride on the four-sixty with him. It was tremendous fun to sit on the red fender, right next to Dad, while the wind blew through my hair and Needles trotted beside us.

"Why are you standing on the stepladder, Daddy?"

My father grabbed the green bottle and tossed it in my direction.

I reached out with both hands and caught it upside down. I turned it upright and saw the letters T-u-r-t-l-e-W-a-x printed on the label.

Turtle Wax?

"You're *waxing* the four-sixty?" I said.

Dad pulled another rag out of his back pocket. "Yup."

Now that I was close to the tractor, I could smell the wax, a bittersweet odor which reminded me of peach pits. Every summer, Mom would buy a couple boxes of peaches to can. Homemade canned peaches tasted much better than the canned peaches from the store.

Several used rags occupied the little shelf on the front of the stepladder where Dad or my brother or sister put paint cans when they were painting. The shelf was knobby with drips of dried paint. Most of the drips were white because all of our farm buildings were white, although light blue drips from the kitchen and pale yellow drips from the living room were mixed in with the white drips.

I looked down at the bottle again. "But I thought this was for cars. And trucks."

Dad folded the rag and continued polishing. "Yes, I guess it is."

"Then why are you using it on the tractor?"

Ingman waxed his car a couple of times a year, and Loretta waxed her car as well. But I had never seen Dad wax anything.

"I wanted to get this done before I start the field work," he said, "to help protect the paint."

"Protect the paint? From what?"

"The sun," he explained. "Sun's hard on the paint. Fades it."

I had to admit the tractor did look nice. The red parts were shiny, like an apple that's been polished, and the white parts looked as clean as puffy clouds drifting across a blue summer sky.

"The sun would fade the paint?" I asked. "Like the sun faded Mom's curtains in the living room?"

The curtains had been white with gold and brown patterns that looked like leaves drifting to the ground on a warm fall day. Mom said she bought the curtains because they were pretty and were made of heavy cotton and would be easy to wash. Except that after the first summer, the curtains didn't have gold and brown patterns anymore. They were mostly just white with light brown streaks.

Mom said the streaks made her curtains look dirty, so the curtains had been replaced with something she called 'drapes' that were the color of ripe corn kernels. Yellow was my mother's favorite color. Mom said if the sun faded her new drapes she was going to give up and leave the living room windows bare.

By the smile on Dad's face, I could tell he clearly remembered the episode with Mom's curtains.

"Yes, kind of like that," he replied.

He reached into his back pocket, pulled out another rag and held it up.

It was a piece of Mom's curtains.

"Mom's letting you use her *curtains* to wax the tractor?"

"Well, I don't know if she knows I'm using them to wax the tractor. They're not much good for curtains anymore, but they make dandy wiping rags."

My father rubbed a few more spots on the engine cowling. Then he climbed off the stepladder and stood back to admire his handiwork before moving around to the front so he could polish the silver ornament at the top of the grill.

In the dazzling April sunlight, the four-sixty looked brand new.

A breeze rustled the maple branches arched high above our heads. The maples didn't have leaves yet, but they were covered with fuzzy red buds that would soon turn into leaves. One of our cows bellowed from the other side of the barnyard fence. "Mooooooo!" she said.

I turned toward the barn. Some of the cows were standing by the fence, watching us.

Dad saw the cows too. "I guess they know it's almost time for their supper, don't they."

He pulled the rags out of his back pocket. "Since they all seem to be expecting it, I suppose I'd better put them in the barn and feed them. And you should probably go in the house and change out of your school clothes."

"Okay, Daddy," I said.

"What's Dad doing?" Mom asked when I walked into the kitchen a few minutes later. She sat by the kitchen table with a cup of coffee and an oatmeal cookie and the newspaper spread out in front of her. We had lots of newspapers at our house. One that came once a week, and one that came every day. Mom was reading the one that came every day.

"How did you know I was talking to Dad?" I asked as I set my books on the table.

"When you didn't come in the house right away, I poked my head out the door to see where you were," she replied.

I might have known. My mother hardly ever missed anything that I did around the place.

"Dad just got done waxing the tractor," I said.

"Dad's waxing the four-sixty?"

"With Turtle Wax. And he used your curtains."

Mom frowned. "My curtains? What in the world is he doing using my curtains?"

She paused. "Oh—you mean the curtains I put into the rag bag. I knew he was doing something with the tractor, but I didn't know he was waxing it."

The hollow feeling in the pit of my stomach suddenly reminded me I still had not yet eaten a snack. "What's for supper?"

"Meatballs and gravy and mashed potatoes," Mom said. "I suppose you're hungry right now, though, aren't you."

"I'm starving."

She turned to look at the clock. "I don't think you're starving in the literal sense, but we won't eat for at least an hour, so I suppose a couple of cookies would be all right."

Last weekend Loretta had baked a batch of oatmeal cookies. She often baked cookies on Sunday afternoons, and this time she had added coconut to the oatmeal cookies.

I finished my cookies and went upstairs to change my clothes, and then a little while later, Dad came in the house.

"I hear you've been doing your spring cleaning," Mom said.

"My spring cleaning?" Dad replied. "Yes, I suppose you could say that. We paid good money for the big tractor and it doesn't hurt to keep it looking nice."

"I also heard you used my curtains."

"They're not much good for curtains anymore," Dad said.

My mother sighed. "No, they're not."

Dad grinned. "Especially not since you ripped them up into rags."

Mom made her way to the table, grasping the back of one of the kitchen chairs to keep her balance. It wasn't so much that my mother sat down. She collapsed. The polio hadn't left her legs with enough strength to allow her to sit down gracefully.

"Roy," she said to Dad after she had settled into her chair, "since when do you have time to wax the tractor, of all things?"

My father lifted one shoulder in a brief shrug. "What else am I going to do on a beautiful spring day when I can't get out in the field yet? Those curtains were just what I needed to do the job. If you don't mind, I'd like to keep them in the shed to use for polish rags."

"Well," Mom said, "I'm glad to hear my curtains are good for *something*."

Although that was the first time I saw Dad waxing the tractor, it certainly wasn't the last. In the following years on the first nice spring day, he would get the four-sixty out to wax it before he started the field work.

Every year, Mom and Loretta did their spring cleaning, too, washing walls and windows and curtains in the kitchen, the living room, the bathroom and all three bedrooms.

From what I could see, Dad had more fun than Mom and Loretta.

Instead of cleaning the curtains—he used the curtains to do his cleaning.

****

~ 4 ~
Mystery of the White Cat

Even though the nights still turned cold enough so the ground was covered with frost in the morning, the days were becoming much warmer, and this evening, for the first time since last fall, Dad had left the barn door open during milking. In the winter, Dad kept the door closed both day and night, but when he left the door open during the evening, that meant spring had finally arrived.

"Would you get the milk stool for me?" Dad asked.

My father used the milk stool to sit by cows who were touchy about the milker.

I turned to fetch the milk stool.

Not more than a minute ago, the doorway had been empty.

But now, a pure white cat sat silhouetted against the gathering dusk beyond.

"Dad," I said. "Look."

My father stepped into the center aisle. As the days grew longer, the cows were shedding more of their winter coats, and the front of Dad's denim chore jacket was covered with black and white hairs.

"Where'd she come from?" he wondered.

I was wondering the same thing myself.

Most of our cats were brown tabbies. "Tiger cats" we called them. The others were either black or gray. We didn't have any white cats. Our elderly neighbors, Hannah and Bill Paulson, had inherited some cats when they bought the farm below our hill several years ago, but none of theirs were white. And Hannah and Bill's cats never came to our place for a visit. Why would they? Hannah fed them canned cat food that smelled like tuna fish, and when she tapped a can with a fork, cats would come running from all directions.

"Forget about the milk stool," Dad said. "If you walk down there now, you'll probably scare the cat away."

Needles had noticed the white cat too. His head was down, his ears were perked, and the tip of his plumed tail was motionless. Every now and then, a stray cat would show up in the barn. If it was a tom, Needles would chase it away. He knew stray toms would fight with our cats, and the dog hated cat fights. As soon as the growling and hissing started, he would wade right in to break it up.

The white cat sat quietly by the door, watching our barn cats as they jostled for position around their dish. The cat dish was an old stainless steel frying pan that my big brother had scrubbed when he washed the milkers until it was as shiny as a new fifty-cent piece. Dad had put more fresh milk in the dish a few minutes ago.

One by the one, the barn cats drank their fill and left the dish to sit and wash their faces or to curl up for a nap in the empty cow stall nearby.

Finally, when the dish was unoccupied, the white stray crept forward, keeping a wary eye on the other cats.

"Looks like she's gonna have kittens," Dad said.

Now that he mentioned it, I could see the white cat was rather plump around the middle.

"More kittens!" I said happily, turning toward my father.

Dad scowled back at me.

"Yeah," he replied, "that's just what we need around here."

In spite of his expression and the gruff-sounding words, Dad was trying not to smile. My father sometimes grumbled about how many barn cats we had, but his attempts to hide a smile often gave him away.

At the other end of the barn, the white cat crouched over the dish, lapping daintily and raising her head every few seconds to look around. After she realized nobody was going to bother her, she drank steadily, as if she hadn't seen anything to eat in a long time.

"Poor kitty," Dad said. "Looks like she's really hungry."

"Do you think she would let me pet her?" I asked.

My father reached for the washcloth so he could prepare the next cow for the milker. As Dad sloshed around in the galvanized bucket, the same kind of bucket we used to feed calves, the scent of iodine rose in a cloud of steam. The disinfectant he used wasn't pure iodine, but it smelled like iodine.

"I don't know if she would let you pet her," he said. "She might. There's only one way to find out, I guess."

I started toward the newcomer, but when the cat noticed my approach, she ran outside, glancing over her shoulder as she disappeared into the dusk of early evening.

I peeked around the door and saw that she hadn't gone far so I retreated into the barn.

Halfway down the barn aisle on my way back toward Dad, I turned around to look. The white cat was by the dish again.

"Any luck?" my father asked, setting down a full bucket of milk. The stainless steel milker inflations clinked and clanked as he placed the cover on an empty bucket.

"She ran away," I said.

Dad turned toward the door where the cat was crouched by the dish. "Didn't go far, I see."

"Daddy? Do you think she will stay here?"

"Who knows? Maybe. Or she might just be passing through."

The next night, the white cat once again appeared in the barn during milking.

And she showed up the night after that.

And the next night.

During the first couple of days, the cat stayed near the door while we milked, although as long as we didn't try to pet her, she didn't mind that we were in the barn. Even if we came quite close to her, she wouldn't run off. And yet, as soon as Dad or I leaned toward her with an outstretched hand, she would either zip out the door or would climb up on the calf pen to put herself out of reach.

After the first night, Needles ignored the white cat. He knew she wasn't going to pick any fights so he had stopped worrying about her.

When the white cat had been at our place for a full week, Dad figured we had acquired a new cat.

"She's been staying in the barn during the day too," he said. "Sleeps in one of the stalls toward the far end."

One evening a few weeks later, the stray arrived at the cat dish looking strangely thin. And I knew what that meant. When a cat was plump with kittens one day but skinny the next, it meant she'd had her babies.

Several days after that, while Dad was in the haymow throwing down hay for the cows before supper, he saw the white cat slip into a hole between the bales. When we came back to the barn after supper, she was sitting on the calf pen.

"Let's see if we can find those kittens before we start to milk," Dad said. "If we go up to the mow while she's down here, maybe she won't realize what we're doing."

The haymow was only a third full. By the time Dad started baling in June, the mow would be nearly empty. The white cat's nest was in a stack of hay along the north wall, and we found three babies all together, two gray ones, and oddly enough, a solid black. They were so tiny that from nose to tail, they fit in the palm of my father's hand.

As Dad put the last kitten back in the nest, the white mother cat appeared. She arrived the way we did: by climbing the haymow ladder. The ladder came up through a hole in the mow floor where Dad and Ingman threw hay down into the barn. During the winter, a sliding door was pulled shut over the hole to help the barn below stay warmer.

"Shoot," Dad said. "I was hoping she wouldn't come up here."

The cat leaped from the ladder to the floor and then jumped on a bale not far away and sat down. She watched us closely with her amber-green eyes. When we headed toward the ladder, she left the bale and went to her nest.

"That's it," Dad said, sounding gloomy. "I bet she's gonna move 'em now."

Most of our cats were tame, but sometimes we wouldn't find a litter of kittens. After their mothers brought them down from the mow, the kittens would scamper away and hide—often behind the big wooden feed box where Dad and I couldn't reach them. As adults, they would remain skittish, and when they had litters of their own, if we found the nest, then they would promptly move their babies to a new place.

Since cats that had been born on our farm who were afraid to be petted would move their babies if we found the nest, then the white cat most definitely would.

The next evening Dad and I went up to the haymow to see if the kittens were still in the same spot.

And much to our surprise, they were.

When three or four days had gone by and the white momma still hadn't moved her babies, Dad concluded she would leave them there.

Not long after that, I decided the stray needed a name. If she had babies upstairs, she belonged here. And if she was our cat, then she had to have a name.

"Daddy? What do you think we should name the white cat?" I asked one evening while we were doing chores.

"What about 'Milky,'" he said. "Or better yet, 'Milkshake.'"

Milky was out of the question, although Milkshake would have been a good name for a white cat who did funny things, such as playing with a string dangling out of the twine barrel. One of our other cats could amuse himself for a long time by batting at a twine string then going around to the back of the barrel, crouching, his haunches working up and down as he prepared to spring, and then dashing around to the front so he could pounce at the twine again. But I had never seen the white cat do anything like that.

"Daa-aad," I said. "What kind of a name is Milky?"

He shrugged. "Well, she's white, and so is milk."

I shook my head.

"Milkshake?" he asked.

I explained that Milkshake would be a good name for a cat who did funny things, like when Tommy played with the twine.

Dad nodded. "I think you're right."

We both remained quiet for a few minutes as my father checked the milker and then pulled it off the cow.

"I know," he said. "Let's call her Kitty."

"Daddy! That's what she is—a cat!"

He picked up the milker and carried it to the next cow.

In the blink of an eye, the perfect name came to me.

"Katherine!" I exclaimed, snapping my fingers.

My father looked up at me from his crouched position. "Katherine? What kind of name is that?"

"It's an *elegant* name."

"WHAT kind of a name?"

"An elegant name. Elegant is one of our spelling words this week, and it means that something is especially nice. She's not an ordinary cat, you know. We don't have any other white ones."

"Well," Dad said, repositioning his blue-and-white pin-striped chore cap, "I suppose Katherine isn't all *that* bad."

And so we began calling the stray white cat Katherine.

Toward the middle of June, when the kittens had gotten their eyes open and had grown big enough to venture out of the nest on their own, Dad said he wouldn't be surprised if Katherine moved her babies after I began playing with them. Sometimes even our tame cats would move their kittens once I started playing with them, he pointed out.

Dad had told me a long time ago that it was important not to play with kittens until they were big enough to leave the nest. "I know you wouldn't hurt them on the purpose," he'd said. "But when they're small, they can't take much handling. And we want our kittens to grow up to be big strong cats. Because if they don't grow up, then who's going to hunt mice for us?"

For the most part, I wasn't afraid of mice, but one day when I was in the granary with Ingman, a mouse had run over my foot. It was an experience I didn't care to repeat.

After I started playing with Katherine's kittens, however, she still did not move them. Often the snow-white cat would sit on a hay bale, watching, while the four of us played my favorite games: follow-the-leader, chase-the-twine-string, and peek-a-boo. The kittens especially liked follow-the-leader and soon learned to come when I called "kitty, kitty."

A few weeks later, Katherine brought her babies down to the barn so they could eat from the dish with the other cats. Katherine also started bringing mice into the barn for her kittens. The mice were very much alive, and when she set them down in front of her kittens, they would chase the mice around the barn. More often than not, the mice would get away.

"Daddy? Why do cats do that? Bring mice in and then let them go?" I asked one day when Katherine's kittens were chasing a mouse, and it scurried out the hole in the wall where the barn cleaner went up a ramp so it could empty into the manure spreader.

"She's teaching her kittens to hunt. That's how they learn," Dad explained.

Even though Katherine devoted many hours to hunting, she was always in the barn during milking. If Dad and I petted or held her kittens, she stayed nearby, but if we tried to pet her, she would jump on the calf pen to get away. As soon as our attention was turned elsewhere, she would come creeping back to sit near the cat dish.

By the time September arrived, I had become so accustomed to seeing Katherine around the barn during chores that one Saturday morning when I didn't see her, I noticed right away she was missing.

I looked in all the usual spots where she liked to nap or to sit and wait for more milk. I couldn't find her anywhere.

"Daddy, have you seen Katherine?" I asked.

He glanced at me and then looked toward the cat dish. "No, I guess I haven't seen her."

"But Katherine's always here at milking time," I said.

Dad shut off the vacuum valve and then grabbed for the milker before it could slide off the cow's udder and onto the floor.

"Don't worry," he said. "She's probably out hunting rats."

Not only did Katherine catch mice, but once she had also caught a rat. I had never seen a rat before, and I was surprised by how much bigger and uglier they were than mice. Dad said he didn't even know we *had* any rats.

"Do you really think that's what's she's doing? Hunting?" I asked.

Dad stepped into the aisle and set the milker on the floor. "She'll be back by tonight. Just you wait and see. In fact, I bet she'll be here when I put the cows in this evening," he said.

But that evening, the white cat did not appear.

And not the next day.

Or the next.

After she had been gone for one whole week, I began to lose hope.

"Daddy, do you think Katherine will ever come back? Or do you think something happened to her?" I asked as he rinsed out the milker buckets after we had finished the evening chores.

Dad stopped to look at me. "She left, I think. Raised her kittens and then went back to wherever she came from."

I stared at my father in disbelief. "Why would she leave? She belongs here."

"Some cats are like that," he said. "They don't want to stay at any one place for very long. Katherine's got her own ideas about where she wants to live. We can't make her stay here, you know."

"But why would she leave some other place, come here and have her kittens and then go back again?"

"Maybe she knew her kittens wouldn't be safe at home," Dad said.

My father picked up the milker bucket and went outside to dump the rinse water on a long, narrow space close to the barn wall. Dad said the water kept the ground damp so we would know where to find worms if we wanted to go fishing in the evening after the chores were done.

I followed him outside.

"What do you mean, her kittens might not be safe at home?" I said.

Dad sloshed the water around and emptied the bucket.

"Well, some people don't want kittens around." He hesitated, and I wondered why his blue eyes looked so troubled. "When a cat has kittens, they…ah…they'll do something like …drown them."

I was so shocked that for a few seconds, I couldn't think of anything to say.

"Daddy! There aren't people who do that. Are there?"

He paused before answering. "Yes, kiddo, I'm afraid so."

"But what about the momma cat?"

Several years ago one of our barn cats had a litter of kittens early in the spring. It had turned cold that same night and the kittens all died. Dad wrapped them in old burlap bag and buried them by the corncrib. For a couple of days, the momma kitty wandered around the barn, calling for her kittens. The longer she looked for them, the more croaky her voice became, until at the end, when she had finally given up, she could hardly meow anymore.

"What about the momma cat?" Dad replied.

"If somebody killed her kittens, wouldn't she be looking for them?"

Dad hesitated again and now his eyes were sad. "Yes—the momma would be looking for them."

"And…and…you think that's why Katherine came here?" I asked. "Because she knew we wouldn't hurt her babies?"

"Could be. Animals are awful smart that way, knowing where they're welcome and where they're not. And we know her kittens will be all right here, don't we."

He winked, and I found myself smiling back at him.

We walked into the barn, and one of Katherine's kittens was sitting near the cat dish. I picked up the young cat I had named Pearl, and she began to purr, a rumbling sound I had no trouble hearing now that the milker pump had been shut off.

Dad chuckled and stroked Pearl's head. "See? I think this is exactly why Katherine came here to have her babies."

Maybe so, although I still didn't understand why she would want to leave.

Not long after that, my father asked around the neighborhood to find out if anybody owned a white cat.

No one did.

He eventually concluded that the question of where Katherine came from was a mystery we would never be able to solve.

By the end of October, I knew Pearl and Silver and Midnight's mother was never coming back. But that didn't stop me from thinking about her, and after a while, I wondered if Dad had made up the story about Katherine coming here to have her babies and then going 'home' after her kittens were grown up because he knew something had happened to her and didn't want to tell me.

But what could have happened to her?

Maybe Katherine got a hit by a car. Although getting hit by a car seemed unlikely since cars hardly ever drove past our place.

Maybe she got run over by the milk truck.

And yet, that didn't seem likely, either, seeing as the milk truck driver always checked under the truck before he drove off.

Or maybe Katherine had gotten into a fight with a wild animal. Perhaps a fox or an owl or a hawk had killed her…

When spring arrived the following year, I had stopped wondering what had happened to Katherine. Pearl and Silver and Midnight were full-grown cats with thick, soft fur, and whenever I picked them up, they would close their eyes and bump their heads against my chin.

One evening after Dad had filled a pail with milk for me so I could carry it to the milkhouse to dump it, I turned toward the door—and stopped dead in my tracks.

"Daddy!" I yelled.

"What's wrong?" Dad replied, as he stepped into the center aisle.

I pointed toward the other end of the barn.

"Well…I'll be…" Dad said.

A white cat was sitting by the cat dish. It was Katherine.

Seconds later, my father and I both arrived at the dish.

"Where have you been?" Dad asked.

"Katherine!" I said. "You're alive!"

"Meowrrr," replied the cat.

At first, I thought the white cat was going to let Dad pet her. But then she scooted out of reach.

"Still afraid of being petted, I see," Dad said, straightening up. "You know we won't hurt you, though. Don't you?"

"Where do you think she was all this time, Daddy?"

"Like I told you before. I think she went back to where she came from after she'd raised her kittens and knew they would be safe."

My father turned and went to check on the milkers.

I trailed along behind him, thinking about what he had said.

For as long as I could remember, we'd had barn cats. Each year at least one, but usually two or three, would have a litter of kittens.

"Daddy?"

"What kiddo?"

"If some people drown kittens, what about mice? Don't they have a lot of mice, then?"

After all, Dad *did* say we wanted our kittens to grow up to be big, strong cats so they could catch mice. And Katherine *did* teach her kittens how to hunt.

"Yes, they've probably got quite a few mice," Dad replied. He winked. "They might even have a few rats."

The white cat was still sitting by the dish, waiting for some milk.

"Daddy? Is Katherine going to have kittens again?"

My father looked at Katherine.

"Yup. I think she's gonna have kittens," he said.

He looked back at me and I wondered why he was smiling in the way my mother called his 'cat that swallowed the canary smile.' When Dad was particularly pleased, he wore the same little grin.

"Yup, I think she's gonna have kittens," he repeated. "And then instead of catching mice for those other people—"

In an instant I saw what he was getting at.

"She'll catch mice here! And maybe even a rat!"

"Well," Dad said, "I really hope there aren't any more rats for her to catch."

A few weeks later, Katherine did, indeed, have another litter of kittens. This time she had two white ones and two brown tabbies. And just like the year before, she caught mice for them. And just like the year before, in the fall, she disappeared.

We never saw her again.

But even though we still had no idea where the white cat had come from or why she came to our farm in the first place, we knew one thing for certain.

All of Katherine's kittens turned out to be the best mousers we ever had.

****

~ 5 ~
May-Day!

The school bus had long since disappeared over the last hill toward the main road one afternoon when I set my books on the kitchen table and hurried into the living room to talk to my mother. Mom was sitting in her favorite easy chair by the picture window, and her crutches were laid neatly on the floor next to the chair where she could reach them.

Outside the window, the air was so clear everything shimmered and sparkled. The fence posts. The plum trees. The lilacs. But even though the sun was shining and the grass was as green as the bottle of food coloring in the kitchen cupboard, a chilly wind blew out of the west. I would never tell her so, but I was glad my mother had insisted I put on my red button-down sweater before I left for school this morning.

"Mom?" I said. "Is it all right if I ride my bike?"

She looked up from the newspaper and peered at me through her black-rimmed reading glasses.

"You won't have much time before supper," she said. "Why don't you go out and find Dad instead?"

Since there were no other children in the family for me to play with, and no neighbor children close by, going outside to see Dad was even more fun than riding my bike.

There was only one problem.

"Isn't he in the field someplace?" I asked.

For the past month, Dad had been plowing, disking and planting. He often didn't arrive home until it was time to put the cows in the barn and feed them. If Dad was out in the field, then he would be too busy to talk to me.

My mother shook her head. "He's finished with the fieldwork. He came in for coffee this afternoon for the first time in I don't know how long."

"Yipee!" I said.

Mom smiled and went back to reading the newspaper.

A little while later after I had changed out of my school clothes and had put on my denim chore coat, I opened the porch door and saw our old, battered, green pickup truck backed up by the granary.

The driveway made a circle past the buildings, and in the middle sat the garage, a round, wooden grain bin, and the red gasoline barrel shaded by a large silver maple. Another silver maple grew in the front lawn, and a row of silver maples lined the lawn in back of the house. One time Mom told me the silver maples had been planted by my great-grandfather.

The granary, which had little windows in the peak near the roof that looked like a square tipped on end, stood across the driveway from the gas barrel. The position of the pickup truck told me that Dad was inside the granary, loading oats into burlap bags, and that he planned to go into town tomorrow to grind feed. About once a week he loaded the truck and made a trip to the feed mill.

I stood on the porch and watched as Dad lifted a burlap bag of oats into the back of the truck. My father made it look as though the bag of oats weighed no more than a ten-pound bag of sugar, but I knew better. A bag of oats weighed about a hundred pounds. Dad had put one on a scale once so I could see how much it weighed.

My father disappeared into the granary again, and I smiled to myself, happy in the knowledge that I knew right where he was, so I wouldn't have to wander around the buildings, yelling for him.

I sat down on the porch steps. All afternoon, the concrete steps had been soaking up sunshine, and beneath the seat of my jeans, the top step felt almost hot. Dandelions filled the lawn, as if someone had scattered handfuls of gold coins, and big, white clouds that looked like giant cotton balls floated across the sky, pushed by the wind.

Only a few days of school remained, and I could hardly wait for summer vacation to begin. We usually got out of school the third week of May if we didn't have too many snow days to make up. And on the last day of school, we always had a picnic. Everybody took their plates outside, and we sat on the grass instead of eating in the cafeteria.

I wasn't looking forward to the picnic quite as much as I did other years, though. Last year on the last day of school, I had no more than settled down with my plate when a garter snake had slithered out between my feet. The mere thought that I had almost sat on a snake still made my stomach do flip-flops.

As I sat there thinking about the school picnic, one of the barn cats came to sit beside me. She had been sprawled in the grass, sunning herself, and beneath my hand, her brown tabby fur felt warm and soft.

In a couple of minutes, the cat went back to sunning herself, and I headed for the rope-and-board swing hanging from the clothesline poles. While cloud shadows slipped across the fields, I swung higher and higher, my arms wrapped around the thick rope tied over the crosspiece. The rope had come from an extra coil stored in the haymow. Dad used the same kind of rope for letting the big door down so he could put hay into the barn during the summer.

When I had gone as high as I could go, I sat quietly while the swing moved slower and slower and slower. More puffy clouds drifted across the sun, and in the field behind the barn, clumps of alfalfa rippled in the cold breeze. The thought crossed my mind that maybe I should have put on a stocking cap. But then reason prevailed. It was May, after all.

I hopped out of the swing and strolled toward the granary just as Dad brought another bag of oats and heaved it into the truck.

The maple trees around the lawn were now covered with green leaves, and as I passed beneath the maple tree by the gas barrel, I was close enough to the truck to see the crack in the upholstery on top of the seat behind the steering wheel.

I had no more than lifted my foot to take another step toward the truck when I noticed something out of the corner of my eye.

I looked down.

And there, coiled in the grass by my feet, was the biggest snake I had ever seen.

I had come within inches of stepping on it.

The snake watched me with beady black eyes—and then its forked tongue flickered in my direction.

Before I had time to think, I drew a deep breath…turned…and took off for the house.

As I raced past the garage, I became aware of someone screaming. Blood curdling screams that were enough to make the hair stand up on the back of my neck.

Then I realized the screams were coming from me.

Seconds later, I cleared the porch steps in one leap and barged into the kitchen, startling my mother, who, by this time, had left the living room.

"What's wrong? Are you hurt?" Mom gasped, as she turned away from the sink.

"Snake!" was all I could say before collapsing against her.

Mom grabbed the cupboard to steady her balance and then put her arm around me. "Where was the snake, honey?" she asked, patting my back with one hand as she held onto the kitchen counter with the other. "Did you see a little grass snake?"

Before I could answer, I heard the porch door open and then the kitchen door.

It was Dad.

"What's wrong?" he asked, sounding slightly breathless. "What happened? Is she hurt?"

"She saw a snake, that's all," Mom replied.

I still had my face pressed tightly against her, but I thought she sounded exasperated.

"It was a BIG snake," I sniffled.

Hah! I wondered how calm Mom would be if *she* had almost stepped on a fifty-foot boa constrictor. We had learned about boa constrictors in science class, and even the smaller ones could eat rabbits in one swallow.

"Oh," Dad said. "I thought maybe she'd hurt herself." He quietly closed the kitchen door and went back outside to finish loading oats.

As I stood there leaning against my mother, I became aware that she was trembling.

I took a step back.

Mom wasn't trembling.

She was laughing—laughing so hard she had tears in her eyes.

I drew a shaky breath. "What's so funny?"

"Hee-hee," she spluttered. "Tee-hee."

"It is NOT," I said, drawing myself up to my full height, "funny."

Mom nodded her head. "Yes, it is."

She made her way over to the table and sat down.

Wouldn't you just know it. I was almost dragged away and killed by the biggest snake I had ever seen, and all my mother could do was laugh. Now that I'd had time to think about it, the snake by the granary was at least as long as the handle of the push broom we used to sweep the barn aisle.

I was beginning to wonder if my mother was ever going to stop laughing when she finally started to wipe her eyes.

"What," I asked once again, "is so funny?"

"Your poor father," she said, as fought back another snicker "There he was, outside minding his own business…and then…well…"

Dad? My mother was laughing because…?

She was laughing because Dad must have run to the house as fast as I did. If not faster.

The thought of Dad running almost made me forget about the snake.

I had never seen Dad run anywhere. Sometimes he walked pretty fast. But I'd never seen him run.

"He probably wondered if you fell out of the tree and broke your arm, or something," Mom explained.

"Oh," I said.

In a little while after I calmed down, I ventured outside again.

The truck was still parked in the same place, but this time, I approached the granary with extreme caution.

I even squatted down to look under the pickup truck.

I didn't see the snake anywhere.

Not in the grass.

Not by the truck.

And not by the granary step.

Then, and only then, did I consider it safe to squeeze past the tailgate and climb into the granary.

"Hi, Daddy," I said, waiting for my eyes to adjust after the bright sunshine outside.

"That was a bull snake," Dad said while he continued bagging oats.

My father had a funny way, sometimes, of knowing what I was going to ask before I could say it—except that knowing what kind of snake it was didn't make me feel any better.

"He's a good snake," Dad added. "I've seen him around here a lot. He helps us. He hunts mice, like the kitties hunt mice. We want him to be around the granary."

"He's a *good* snake?"

As far as I was concerned, there was no such a thing as a 'good' snake.

"Will he bite?" I asked.

I had watched the cats hunt mice, and I understood why Dad didn't want mice in the granary. He said the cows wouldn't eat the feed if it had mouse droppings in it. I didn't blame them. Who would want to eat something that had mouse droppings in it?

"No," Dad said, dumping another shovel of oats in the bag, "the snake won't hurt you. I suppose he was taking a sunbath when you saw him. The sun is warm today, but that wind is awfully chilly."

By now, I was starting to feel a tiny bit guilty about my terrified, screaming reaction to the snake. If my father said he was a good snake—and that he was only taking a sunbath, just like the kitty by the porch had been taking a sunbath—then maybe it wasn't quite so bad.

"Tell you what," Dad continued, using a short section of string to tie the bag shut with a miller's knot, "whenever you're around the granary, keep an eye out for the bull snake. That way, the next time you see him, he won't be so scary."

"Are you sure he won't bite?" I asked.

Dad heaved the full bag of oats into the truck.

"No, kiddo," he said. "The snake won't bite. In fact, I'd even be willing to bet that *you* scared him more than he scared you."

I seriously doubted the snake had been more scared than me, but I kept it to myself.

For a long time after that, whenever I went near the granary, I looked for the bull snake.

But I never saw him again.

And neither did Dad.

"What do you suppose happened to that snake, Daddy?" I asked one day a few weeks later when he was loading oats again.

"I think you scared him away," Dad said, taking another burlap bag and hooking it over a nail to hold up one side while he shoveled oats into it. "He probably decided to go live someplace else where it was quieter."

"Do you *really* think he moved?" I asked. "Just because of that?"

My father nodded solemnly. "Snakes don't want to be where there's a lot of commotion. You wouldn't like it if someone screamed just because they saw you, would you?"

I thought about that for a few moments.

"No, Daddy. I wouldn't like it."

I hoped, then, that the snake had found a nice place to live, a quiet place where his afternoon sunbath wouldn't be interrupted by blood-curdling screams of terror.

And with any luck at all, it would also be someplace where I wouldn't almost step on him again.

****

6

An Alternate Route

We were part way through the milking one evening when Dad pointed to the door that opened into the barnyard. "There she goes again," he said.

A minute later, the barn swallow flew back through the doorway. This time she was carrying a lump of mud in her beak.

"Now watch what she does," Dad said.

Every year, four or five pairs of barn swallows came to live in our barn, and each pair often raised two sets of babies before they left in September. After the young ones were big enough to leave the nest, they would perch on the top wire of the barnyard fence to rest in between practice flights.

The barn swallows were pretty birds, dark blue above, like the night sky half an hour after sunset, and pale, rosy orange below, although some were more the color of cream rather than rosy orange. The swallows had forked tails, and they looked as if someone had trimmed their tail feathers with a sharp scissors. When the swallows sat on their nests near the whitewashed ceiling, they would watch us with bright black eyes as we milked the cows.

I tilted my head back to see the light fixture where the barn swallow had landed so I could watch what she was doing. In front of her was a layer of mud. She added the lump she had brought in with her, and then she flew outside again.

I had never watched a barn swallow build a nest. Not a whole nest. Sometimes I had seen them make repairs, but for as long as I could remember, they had used the same nests, year after year. Except that last fall, while Dad was using a broom to clean cobwebs off the ceiling, he had accidentally hit one of swallow nests and knocked it down.

"Why do they build their nests on top of the lights?" I asked.

"The top makes a good platform for the nest doesn't it?" Dad said.

The white ceramic light fixtures were attached to the ceiling in such a way that part of the top was exposed. I looked up at one of the other nests in the barn. The bottom of the nest rested on the light fixture, and the back was attached to the ceiling joist.

Although it was not dark outside, my father had turned on the barn lights. The sun would set in a little while, and by the time we were done milking, we would need lights on in the barn. From experience with the lamp beside my bed, I knew light bulbs became hot because one day when the bulb went out and I touched it to make sure it was screwed in tightly, the way I had seen my big sister, Loretta, check the bulb, I had burned my fingers.

"But what about the bulb. Doesn't it get hot up there?" I asked.

"Oh, sure, the bulb is warm, but that's what they want," Dad said.

"Why?"

"To help keep the babies warm. When we used to raise baby chicks, we had to put a heat lamp in with them so they wouldn't freeze to death if it got chilly. Baby birds can't stand being cold."

I could barely remember when we had chickens. What I recalled most was a rooster chasing me and trying to peck my legs. I also recalled my mother complaining about chicken manure in the yard.

Then I thought of something else. "Remember when my friend stayed overnight? And she said that her dad wouldn't let swallows live in their barn?"

My father turned to look at me. He was sitting on the milk stool beside a cow to keep an eye on the milker.

"I remember."

"How come you don't knock down the nests?"

Dad's blue eyes seemed even more blue now that his face was deeply tanned from driving the tractor all spring. His blue chambray work shirt was a lighter color across the shoulders where the sun had faded it, and his blue denim overalls were faded at the knees.

"I like having swallows around the barn," he said. "They catch lots of flies."

The cows were standing quietly with only the occasional swish of a tail. Flies would become more of a problem by the middle of the summer. The cows would stomp and kick to chase the flies away, and then Dad would spray the barn with fly spray. The fly spray smelled like used motor oil mixed with glue.

"Sometimes I know it seems like we have quite a few flies," Dad continued, almost as if he knew what I had been thinking, "but I've been in barns that were so thick with 'em, I didn't want to open my mouth to say anything."

"Why was that?" I asked.

"I was afraid I'd get a mouthful flies," Dad said. "I think one of the reasons we don't have that many flies to begin with is because the barn swallows are here."

My father lifted off his cap and settled it more firmly on his head.

"Besides, the swallows have just as much of a right to live their lives as we do to live ours," he said.

The barn swallow flew back into the barn and placed another lump of mud. Each lump only added a small amount to the nest. At this rate, it was going to take her a long time to finish. Maybe even a couple of days.

Dad stepped across the gutter to take the milker off, and then he set the bucket in the middle of the aisle. I could tell from the sound of the thump that the bucket was full.

For the next few minutes I was occupied with carrying pails of milk to the milkhouse to dump them and couldn't watch the barn swallow. The full buckets of milk were too heavy for me to lift, so Dad would fill the milk pail for me. A full milker bucket often meant three trips to the milkhouse.

On my first trip, the barn cats swarmed around my feet, looking at me with hopeful eyes. I stopped by the cat dish to pour some milk into it, and before I had finished pouring, they had already put their noses in the dish.

I finished emptying the milker bucket and went back to watching for the barn swallow. In a little while, she returned with more mud, flew up to her nest, daubed it on, and then flew outside again.

"How do they know how to do that?"

"Do what?" Dad asked as he checked on a cow who was fidgeting. When she moved back and forth in her stall, the milker attached to her udder also swung back and forth.

"How do they know how to build nests?"

With an expert hand, Dad massaged the cow's udder and then shut off the vacuum valve. As soon as he removed the milker, the cow quit fidgeting.

"It's an instinct," he said. "It's something they all carry inside of them, to know how to build nests. When the babies grow up, they'll know how to build nests too."

I had heard Dad talk about instincts before. It was an instinct, he said, for a first-calf heifer to know how to take care of her baby. No one had to teach her. She just knew.

After a few more minutes of watching the barn swallow fly in and out of the barn, I came to a decision.

"I want to see her get the mud," I said to Dad.

My father was in the middle of washing a cow's udder.

"Go through one of the other doors and walk around outside to the barnyard," he said.

The barn had three doors: one on the west end, where the swallow was flying in and out, one on the east end facing the machine shed, and one on the south wall. A silo used to be on the other side of the south door, but it had been torn down years ago.

I looked at Dad and frowned. "Go through one of the other doors? Wouldn't it be easier to go out this door?"

"Oh, sure, it would be easier," he replied. "But Mrs. Swallow might not want to fly back into the barn if you're standing right there."

I did as Dad suggested and left the barn through the silo door. The evening air was filled with the scent of lilacs. Behind the house, three large lilac bushes planted by my grandmother, Inga, were in full bloom. The lilacs had so many flowers that you could hardly see any green leaves on the bushes. I was surprised I could smell the lilacs from here, although once I thought about it, I realized the wind was blowing from that direction.

I arrived in the barnyard just in time to see the swallow fly out of the door. The sun was almost ready to set, and the slanting rays cast an orange glow over the white barn. From the tops of the silver maples around the yard, robins trilled their good-night songs.

The swallow went to a spot near the fence, landed on the ground, picked up some mud, and flew into the barn. I watched her fly back and forth a few times, then I returned to the barn the way I had left.

"Did you see her?" Dad asked.

"A couple of times."

"Did she go to the same spot?"

"Sort of," I said. "She didn't get the mud from the same exact spot, but it was the same area over by the fence."

Dad picked up the milker and moved to the next cow. "Must be good material there. Not too soft and not too dry."

During the time we had been watching her, the barn swallow had added almost two whole layers of mud to her nest, but she was still a long way from done.

"She'll probably have her nest finished by tomorrow night," Dad said, as he hooked up the vacuum line.

"By *tomorrow* night?" I said.

I could see why the barn swallow was working on her nest now, when the cows were in the barn for milking and the door was open. But we would finish milking soon, and then Dad would turn the cows outside for the night. In the morning, he would put the cows in the barn to feed them, and when he had finished milking, he would turn the cows outside again.

And each time after Dad let the cows out, he closed the barn door.

"But—after the cows go outside, we always shut the door. How will the swallow get in and out to the barnyard when the door is closed?" I asked.

"The next time she comes in, go down there and shut the door. Then come back here and watch what happens," he said.

"But, Daddy, if I shut the door, how will she get out?"

"Wait and see."

So, the next time the barn swallow came in to add more mud, I was waiting near the calf pen. As she flew to her nest, I closed the door.

During the few seconds it took me to walk back to where Dad was standing, I had already decided that closing the door was a bad idea. A very bad idea.

Last week, while Mom and I were sitting in the living room one afternoon, we had been surprised by a loud 'thud' when a robin had hit the picture window. Mom said she'd seen a barn cat in the yard a few minutes earlier and that she hoped the robin hadn't knocked himself out and that the cat wouldn't get him. When I went outside to see if the bird was all right, the robin was lying on the ground, dead.

I couldn't get the image of the dead robin out of my mind, and by the time the barn swallow had finished daubing on the mud, I was sure she was about to get killed.

When the swallow left her nest, turned, and went toward the door on the opposite end of the barn, I could hardly believe my eyes. She flew outside and banked to the left, which would take her past the milkhouse and around into the barnyard.

I stared at Dad in open-mouthed astonishment.

"Pretty smart, isn't she," he said.

Even though the door leading into the barnyard would be closed all day, the door on the other end of the barn would be open, or at least the upper half of the door would be open. The barn swallow could fly in and out as she pleased, and if she worked on her nest all day tomorrow, maybe she *would* be finished by tomorrow night.

"How did you know she'd do that?" I asked.

"What would you do if one door was closed but the other was open?" Dad replied.

I didn't even have to think about it.

"I'd go out the door that was open."

"Exactly," Dad said. "You'd take a different route."

But then I had another thought. If the barn swallow was smart enough to avoid flying into the door...

"Why did the robin fly into the window?" I asked.

"Robin? What robin?" Dad said as he took the cover off one milker and put it on an empty bucket.

"Last week a robin hit the picture window."

"How do you know it was a robin?"

"Mom said she'd seen a cat in the yard a little before that, and if the bird had knocked himself out, she was afraid the cat would get him before he woke up. I went outside to see if it was there yet, and it was a robin, but it was dead."

"Are you sure it wasn't just knocked out?" Dad asked.

I had seen enough things that had died—cows and calves and cats—to know dead when I saw it.

"I think it broke its neck when it hit the window."

Dad winced and shook his head. "Poor thing."

"So how come the barn swallow turned around but the robin hit the window?"

My father took the milker to the next cow. "The robin didn't know it was a window. He thought it was an open space he could fly through. The barn swallow could see the door."

A row of windows occupied both sides of the barn in front of the cow stanchions. Some of the windows were made of thick blocks of glass you couldn't see through, but some were made of clear glass.

"Why don't the swallows fly into the barn windows?" I asked.

"Because they can see 'em."

"What do you mean—they can see them?"

Dad grinned. "I don't keep my barn windows as clean as Ma and your sister keep the house windows."

The barn windows made of clear glass weren't exactly clear. They were cloudy with dust from the hay and the ground feed and from the white barn lime Dad sprinkled on the floor.

"Good reason not to wash windows isn't it," Dad said.

To my way of thinking, it was an excellent reason. The last time Mom and Loretta had washed the house windows, my mother insisted that I help too. As I stood on a stepladder outside to wash the kitchen window, Mom had stood on the inside. I thought I was never going to get done with the window because my mother kept pointing out streaks. In all, I had washed the same window three times.

"Daddy?"

"What, kiddo?"

"Do you think I should try to talk Mom and Loretta into not washing the house windows?"

"Why is that?"

"So the robins won't hurt themselves."

After a few moments of silence, we both arrived at same conclusion. "Naaaa…," Dad said, "it'll never work."

Shoot. For just a second there, I thought I'd found a way to save the robins and myself.

Well, at least I no longer had to worry about the barn swallow, since I had seen with my own eyes that she was smart enough to find another way out of the barn.

Now, if only I could find some way to get out of washing more windows…

****

7

A Terrible Life

I had managed to get as far as filling the stock tank half full of water when I noticed a car coming over the first hill by the church. After dinner, Dad had gone to the other place to see if the corn would soon be ready for cultivating, and before he left, he had asked me to fill the tank.

The cows had been back in the pasture all morning, and now, at early afternoon, they were thirsty and had come up to the barnyard for a drink. They arrived at the tank by twos and threes and fours, dipping their noses into the clear, cold water and then raising their heads, ears waggling to chase away the flies, before taking another drink or wandering away to stand in the shade of the barn wall.

The stock tank was on the other side of the milkhouse, just inside the barnyard fence, and while I waited for it to fill, I occupied myself by walking down the driveway to the far corner of the barn and then back again. The sun was almost directly overhead, and the warm sunshine felt good on my bare arms.

It was when I had reached the corner of the barn for the third time that I saw the car. As I stood there watching it, I wondered if it was going to stop at the next-door neighbor's place or if it was coming to our place. We rarely had visitors, and the next-door neighbor's farm and our farm were the only two along our mile-long stretch of road.

A few minutes later, I knew the car was on its way to our place when I heard it coming up the driveway. The car rounded the curve by the willow tree, and I saw it was a black four-door with a man and a woman inside.

"Who do you suppose that is?" I said when I went back to the stock tank to see if it was full yet. It wasn't, of course. For a while, the cows had been drinking faster than the hose could keep up.

Twenty-some sets of dark eyes stared back at me. The cows didn't care whether we had visitors.

I went into the milkhouse to shut off the water. Dad didn't like it when the tank overflowed. He said the barnyard was muddy enough already without adding to the problem. My father was particularly concerned about the tank, I had noticed, ever since he had left the hose on while he went into the machine shed to work on the manure spreader. "Nuts! I forgot all about it," he said, when Mom sent me outside to find out why the water pump had been running for so long.

The car had turned to park near the house, and after I came out of the milkhouse, I couldn't see it since it was on the other side of the garage. To reach the house, I had two choices: walk around the garage by the barn, or walk around the garage the other way by the machine shed.

I headed toward the machine shed. My mother was already coming down the porch steps, bent forward at the waist to help keep her balance, first one crutch down the step, then the other, then one foot, then the other. After the last step, she pushed herself upright, inching the crutches backward until they were beside her. Then she started forward, moving one crutch, then the other, swinging one leg out from the hip, then the other.

The man and the woman were standing beside the car, and I was pretty sure Mom was on her way to invite them into the house. We rarely had company, but when we did, Mom invited visitors to the house for a cup of coffee and a piece of cake or some cookies.

Bees buzzed around the pink petunias planted not far from the front steps, and the scent of baking bread sweetened the air. My mother had put a batch of bread into the oven not long ago, and the aroma had begun to drift out of the open kitchen window.

By the time I made it past the machine shed and the clothesline, my mother was talking to the man and woman.

"Well," the man said, as I came to stand beside Mom, "who is this?"

He was dressed in a pair of dark brown suit pants, a necktie and a white shirt with the sleeves rolled up partway to his elbows. The only place I saw men wearing suit pants, white shirts and neckties was at church on Sunday.

"This is my youngest daughter," Mom replied as she took a firmer grip on her crutches.

"I see," the man said.

Although his face was smiling, his eyes were not smiling. They were flat and hard, the way a cat's eyes become flat and hard when two of them are sitting face to face, staring, tails lashing, and you know that any second, they're going to start a fight.

"Your daughter must be a big help to you," the woman said. She wore a light blue dress and high heels. Big light-blue button earrings were clipped to her earlobes, and her pink lipstick looked as if she had put more on before getting out of the car.

The woman was smiling, too, but in her case, so were her eyes.

"Oh, yes, she's a very big help," my mother said. "She's my legs sometimes."

Mom often asked me to do things for her. Like the day she had sent me outside to find out why the water pump had been running so long.

"I'm sorry you wasted a trip," Mom said, looking back and forth between the man and woman, "but we don't need any more insurance."

The man leaned back against the car and folded his arms.

"Are you sure of that?" he asked. "What about all of your buildings? The machinery? The crops?"

Mom shook her head. "No, we've got enough insurance for the time being, thank you."

"Oh, come now," the man said, standing up straight again. "You can never have *too* much insurance."

"Well, I'm sorry," Mom said, "but we have enough."

Her voice was not quite as friendly as it had been only moments before.

"Maybe we should talk to your husband," the man said. "I'm sure *he* would have a better idea of whether you need more insurance."

The woman put her hand on the man's arm. "We understand about not needing more insurance," she said.

He took a deep breath and blew it out slowly.

"Well," he said, "I suppose maybe you're right."

"It's a beautiful day, isn't it?" the woman said to Mom. "And since it's such a lovely day for a drive, we'll just be on our way to the next place."

The woman turned toward the car, and I thought the man was going to follow her. But then he blurted out a question.

"Would it be all right if I got a glass of water?"

My mother hesitated for only a second before turning toward me. "Would you please show him to the kitchen?"

I wasn't sure that I liked this man well enough to do him any favors, but as long as my mother asked...

The house was quiet except for the songs of robins and Baltimore orioles and the twittering of barn swallows that I could hear through the open kitchen window. Mom's bread smelled like it was almost finished, and in a short while, I knew I would be eating a slice of fresh hot bread with butter and sugar and cinnamon.

I got a glass out of the cupboard, filled it with water from the tap and handed it to the man. He drained it in one swallow and set the empty glass on the counter.

"How long," he said in a low voice as he glanced out the kitchen window, "has your mother been like that?"

He bent forward and peered at me intently.

"How long has she been like what?" I replied.

"Using crutches," he said. "How long has she been a cripple?"

Sometimes the kids at school asked me how long Mom would have to walk with crutches and whether she would ever get better, but I'd never had an adult ask me about it.

"I'm not sure," I said. "Since before I was born."

The man shook his head. "What a terrible life," he said. "Why—if I was crippled up like that, I wouldn't even want to be alive. Sometimes I'll bet she's sorry she was ever born."

He turned and walked out of the kitchen.

Seconds later I heard the screen door click shut.

After awhile when the car started and the sound of the engine was accompanied by the crunch of tires on stones in the driveway, I was still standing there in the kitchen, wondering what he had meant.

Sure, I knew it was difficult for Mom to get around.

And I knew she'd just as soon not have been paralyzed by polio.

But did she have a 'terrible life?'

And was she sorry she had been born?

A few minutes later, my mother returned to the house.

"I'd better see if my bread is done yet," she said, setting her crutches against the table. She grabbed hold of one kitchen chair, then the next one, and then the stove. She opened the oven door, reached inside and flicked her finger against the bread. The sound was both hollow and solid at the same time.

Before dinner, Mom had put the kettle of bread dough on a chair—as she always did when she baked bread—and had stood in front of it, bent forward at the waist, so she could knead the dough. While we ate, the dough had sat in the warm oven to rise. After dinner, she had shaped it into loaves and put it into the oven to rise again.

And now the bread was finished.

I watched as she took four loaves of bread out of the oven and set them on hot pads. She opened the cupboard door, reached for the can of shortening and pulled open a drawer to find a pastry brush.

My mother held onto the counter with her left hand while with her right, she used the pastry brush to dab shortening onto the bread. Brushing shortening on the bread immediately after it was baked, Mom said, kept the crust from drying out.

As my mother dipped the pastry brush into the can of shortening a second time, I couldn't stand it anymore.

"Mom, are you sorry you were born?"

The silver brush clattered to the counter. My mother turned a disconcerted gaze in my direction and pushed her dark curly hair away from her forehead with the back of her hand.

"What on *earth* would make you ask such a question?"

"That man who was here. He said because you had polio you have a terrible life and that he bets you're sorry you were born."

She blinked a couple of times and then her blue eyes narrowed.

"Well," she said crisply, "I don't know what business it is of his, but I can think of things that would be worse."

"Like what?" I asked.

No one had to tell me that having polio wasn't much fun. During the winter, when it was snowy and icy outside, Mom often stayed in the house for several months at a time. She was afraid that if she slipped and fell, she would break an arm or a leg.

But then, when the weather was good, if my mother wanted to go somewhere—shopping or to church or to a Ladies' Aid meeting—she had to wait until my father, sister or brother could take her. Mom's legs would never be strong enough for her to learn how to drive a car.

My mother also couldn't work in the garden or mow the lawn. And she couldn't milk the cows or go for a walk around the farm or run out to open a gate if Dad was ready to drive through with the tractor. And the only way she could go upstairs or to the basement was by crawling on her hands and knees. If she needed to send a letter, she would ask me to take it to the mailbox at the bottom of our driveway. The hill was too steep for her to go up and down with her crutches.

"There are a lot of things worse than polio," my mother continued. "Losing my husband or one of my children in an accident would be much worse. *That* would be terrible."

"It would?" I said.

"Yes, of course it would. I've pretty much lost the use of my legs, but it's nothing compared to losing one of my family."

Mom picked up the silver brush and dabbed more shortening on the bread.

"Does that mean you're not sorry you were born?" I asked.

She stopped and put the brush on the counter, and once again her expression grew stern. "Honestly," she said, "I can't imagine what he was thinking. Saying something like that to a child. If he wanted to find out, he should have asked me."

Then her face softened. "Come here," she said.

I moved closer to my mother.

She looked into my eyes. "There are always going to be people in this world who say stupid things, and when they do, you must consider the source."

"What does that mean?"

"Where it came from—who said it," she explained. "Like that man. He doesn't know anything about me except what he saw in the few minutes they were here. And that was wrong."

"It was?" I said.

"Very wrong. And I would like it if you did not do the same thing. You must try not to judge people on appearances."

"What does that mean? 'Judge people on appearances?'"

"It means," my mother said, "that you can't tell much about people by the way they walk. Or the clothes they wear. Or what color their hair is."

As I picked up the empty glass the man had used and put it in the sink, I thought about what she had said.

"You mean like that time when I was really little and I was afraid of Santa Claus?"

Before I started kindergarten, the country school a mile from our farm where my mother, brother and sister had gone to grade school was still open. Mom and my sister liked to go to the Norton school's Christmas program, and the last year Norton still had classes, before the country schools were combined with the school in town, I had gone to the program with Mom and Loretta. And suddenly, a man wearing a bright red suit and a white beard came up the steps from the front door yelling, "HO! HO! HO!" In my opinion, he looked dangerous. He practically scared me to death, and I was quite sure I didn't like him one bit.

Later on, after I started school, I discovered the man who had played Santa Claus was the custodian at the school in town. His name was Mike Flynn, and he wasn't at all 'dangerous'—he liked to laugh and tease and tell jokes.

I never told anyone, but I was a little ashamed of myself for being afraid of someone as nice as Mike Flynn the first time I saw him.

My mother smiled and picked up the pastry brush again.

"Yes, that's exactly what I mean. You thought the guy who was Santa Claus was an awful person, but you'd never seen him before, so how could you have any idea what he was like?"

Even though I still felt upset because the man who visited our farm had called my mother a cripple and said she had a terrible life, I realized Mom was right. He didn't know a thing about her.

But I did.

And today I learned something else.

All along I had known that my mother loved us. But I never knew we were more important to her than her legs.

"Mom?"

"Yes, what is it?"

"I'm glad you were born."

My mother set the pastry brush on the counter and put her arm around my shoulders.

"Me, too, sweetheart," she said. "Me, too."

****

(A recipe for Norma's Homemade Bread is included in Appendix A.)

~ 8 ~
A Break in the Weather

School had been out for two weeks, but it still seemed strange to me that I could eat breakfast with Mom and Dad. During the school year after I helped my father with the chores, I would come into the house, eat breakfast by myself, get ready for school and then walk down the driveway to meet the school bus.

We wouldn't be eating breakfast for a little while yet, though, not until Dad finished shaving. Most days when my father came in from the barn, he shaved before he ate breakfast. And at the moment, I could tell he wasn't finished yet. The muffled singing from behind the bathroom door gave it away.

"Lie-dee-die-dee-die-dee-doe—lie-dee-diiiiie-dee-doe—lie-dee-die-dee-die-dee-dooooooe…"

"What's he got to sing about, I wonder," Mom said, as she flipped over more pancakes so they could bake on the other side.

The "lie-dee-die" song had no particular melody, not that I could ever figure out. Sometimes Dad sang it while he milked, sometimes while he fixed machinery and sometimes while he shaved. The "lie-dee-die" song was a sure indication Dad was in a good mood and felt especially pleased with himself.

A few minutes later, my father emerged from the bathroom. He had slicked back his hair with a wet comb. Dad's hair was gray on the sides and dark on top. Well, mostly dark on top. And not much hair on top.

I could smell Old Spice aftershave too. My father liked to put on some Old Spice after he finished shaving. He said the cows probably didn't care one way or the other what he smelled like but that he thought the people he lived with would appreciate it.

"What have you got to sing about?" my mother inquired.

Dad went to the stove and poured a cup of coffee for himself.

"Well, for one thing, the sun is shining and there isn't a cloud in the sky. And for another thing, the weatherman on the radio says there's only a slight chance of showers for the next week," Dad said.

He picked up the plate of pancakes Mom had made and set them in the middle of the table.

"Help yourself, kiddo," he said to me. "Eat while you've got the chance because…I'm gonna cut hay today."

'Eat while you've got the chance' was my father's way of saying we would soon be busy with work that might keep us too occupied to eat. It was one of Dad's little jokes. He never missed a meal. "Can't work if you don't eat" was another of his favorite sayings.

"That's what they said on television too, just a slight chance of showers," Mom said. She turned away from the stove and took hold of the nearest chair. "So I suppose it wouldn't hurt to cut a few loads to get started."

Dad shook his head. "I'm planning to cut the whole field."

"Which one?" Mom asked. She carefully lowered herself onto the chair where she always sat, on the opposite side of the table from Dad.

"The field behind the barn," he replied.

"The whole thing?" Mom said, sounding horrified at the very thought.

"Why not? Might as well jump in and get a good start."

In addition to the one-hundred-and-twenty acres homesteaded by my mother's family in the late 1800s, Mom and Dad owned another hundred acres on a second farm about a mile north. The field behind the barn was twenty acres. Dad generally didn't cut twenty acres at a time. Five acres, maybe. Sometimes ten. But not twenty. With only two hay wagons, it took a long time to bale just five acres—a couple of days if the hay was thick.

"The whole thing?" Mom repeated. "Are you sure you should do that?"

"We've gotta start or we'll never finish," Dad said.

"Are you going to cut this morning?" I asked.

He nodded as he pulled out his chair and sat down. "Not much dew today. I want to get a little of it done before dinner."

In a way, I was happy Dad was going to start cutting hay, and in a way, I wasn't. To me, haying meant summer had arrived, once and for all. Except after the first field was cut, it seemed like that's all we did for the rest of the summer was bale hay, going from one field to the next to the next, acre by acre by acre.

Now and again, we would get a short break between finishing the last field of first crop and starting the first field of second crop, and another short break between finishing the last field of second crop and starting the first field of third crop. But a few days here and there didn't seem like much of a break.

"Are you *absolutely sure* you should cut the whole field?" Mom asked as she slid a pancake off the stack and onto her plate.

Dad reached for the clear glass pitcher of pancake syrup. The syrup was made from brown sugar, butter, vanilla, a few tablespoons of water and boiled until it was thick and smooth.

"The weather forecast says we *might* get a little rain. A quick shower won't make much difference," he said.

"You know I don't like to see the hay get wet," Mom said.

"Can't always be helped," Dad replied. "If I waited until I was sure we'd have all sunny days, we'd never start haying. And then where would we be?"

Mom sighed. "I still don't like to see the hay get wet."

"Who says it's going to get wet?" Dad said as he drizzled syrup over his pancakes.

Later that afternoon, my father finished cutting the field west of the house. When Mom went into the kitchen to start making supper, she gazed out the window at the neat swaths of cut hay and shook her head.

The next day, the sun was warm and the sky was clear, all but for a few patches of hazy clouds that looked like the gauzy material my sister used to line a collar when she was sewing a dress or a blouse.

When Dad came in the house for supper, he was whistling. Just like the "lie-dee-die" song, when Dad whistled, he was happy and pleased with himself. But also just like the "lie-dee-die" song, the whistling never had a tune I could recognize.

Dad took off his chore cap and hung it over the newel post. "I think we can start baling tomorrow afternoon," he said.

"So soon?" Mom asked.

She was sitting by the table, waiting for Dad to come in and wash his hands and face so we could eat. The table was set, and supper was in the oven—a casserole made of potatoes and carrots and onions and ground beef.

"Wonderful drying conditions today. Just the right amount of wind and sun. Looks like it'll be some of the best hay we've ever had," Dad said.

My mother frowned, causing a crease to form beside each eyebrow. "Don't talk like that."

"Like what?"

"You'll jinx it."

Dad grinned as he headed for the bathroom to get cleaned up. "You worry too much."

Later the next morning, my father started raking hay. He took a quick break for dinner, and by mid-afternoon, half of the field was raked.

"We'll just let that sit for an hour or so, and then we can start baling," Dad said as he came in the house for a cup of coffee and a cookie. "If we work fast, we'll be able to get two loads off it this afternoon and maybe another load after milking, if the dew doesn't fall too soon."

My big brother, Ingman, was working at the creamery, but this week he worked the 7-to-3 shift, so he would be home soon. When they finished baling, it would be my job to put bales on the elevator while Dad and Ingman stacked hay in the mow. The only part of unloading hay I didn't like was if a snake stuck out of the bale. The snakes were most often black-and-yellow striped garter snakes, but occasionally I saw one that was red-and-black striped.

After going through the baler, the snakes were usually dead, although every once in a while, one would still be alive. Either way, our dog, Needles, would stand on the hay wagon, carefully watching each bale. If he saw a snake, he would yank it out of the hay and shake it and then drop it on the hay wagon.

"Why did you rake so much?" Mom asked while she poured a cup of coffee for herself and one for Dad. "You won't get it all baled today. Shouldn't you have left it until tomorrow?"

"When the neighbors come over tomorrow to help, they'll bring some extra wagons, and this way, we'll be able to start baling right after dinner. Somebody can rake up the rest of it, and while one wagon's being unloaded, the other ones can be out in the field—"

"Shhhh!" Mom said, holding up her hand. "What was that?"

"What was what?" Dad asked.

"Sounded like thunder," my mother replied.

"Now, Ma," he said, setting down his cup of coffee and going to the kitchen window. "Maybe the train had to stop for some reason."

The tracks were a half mile away, and although we couldn't see the train when it passed by because of the hills between our place and the tracks, we could hear the train.

Dad looked out the window for a few seconds, and when he turned around, he wasn't smiling anymore.

"It *was* thunder, wasn't it," Mom said.

My father nodded.

"I KNEW it," she said.

"If it's a quick shower, it'll be all right," Dad said. "As long as the windrows aren't soaked, maybe we'll still be able to bale tomorrow."

A short while later, it started raining. Dad said he had never seen a thundershower come up that quickly.

It didn't turn out to be a quick thundershower, however, because by late afternoon, it was still raining.

And it rained straight through the night.

And all of the next day.

And the next.

And the next.

Not a downpour. Not a stormy rain. Not a windy rain. Just a steady, quiet, light rain.

As each day passed, from the kitchen window, I could see the hay turning from green to light brown to the color of coffee.

So could Dad. Every time he came in the house for breakfast, dinner or supper, he would stand by the window for a few minutes and stare out at the hayfield.

To her credit, Mom did not say, "I told you so." My father was disgusted enough already, so I suppose she decided she didn't have to.

As for the hay, by the time the rain stopped, it wasn't even fit to use for bedding. Dad said hay never made good bedding, but in a pinch, and if he had hay he would rather not feed, he would use it in the calf pens.

"What are you going to do with all of that hay?" Mom asked one morning after the rain had stopped.

Dad shrugged. "Let it dry out for a few days, rake up the rest of it, and then bale it to get it off the field. After that, well...I don't know...throw some of it out in the pasture and let the cows stomp it up, I guess. The rest can go in that washout on the other place. It'll help keep it from getting worse."

My mother didn't look especially happy about throwing away hay, but I think she also knew nothing else could be done with it.

"Boy, were they ever wrong when they said we 'might' get a few showers," Mom said.

Dad rubbed his forehead, the way he did when he had a headache. "If that's what they mean by a few showers, the next time they say it's going to rain, maybe we'd better be like Noah and build an ark."

Of course it wasn't the first time that hay got wet.

And it wasn't the last.

But it was the longest break we had ever gotten from baling hay.

Too bad we hadn't started yet.

****

~ 9 ~
The One and Only

We were almost finished with the evening milking, and a few minutes ago, Dad had asked me to go out and close the gate across the lane and open the gate to the pasture behind the pole shed.

Dad switched the pastures at night to keep the cows closer to the barn so we wouldn't have to walk as far in the morning to find them. If we didn't have to look for the cows, we saved a half an hour doing the chores, which meant we could eat breakfast that much sooner. And I was all for anything that would allow us to eat breakfast sooner rather than later.

The barnyard gates were made of four strands of barbed wire with two small posts in the middle to hold them up. After I had opened the lane gate in the morning, as usual, I had pulled it back and set it against the fence to keep the cows from getting tangled up in it.

On my way across the barnyard, I made sure that I watched where I was putting my feet. Fresh cow pies dotted the ground, and I would just as soon not have to clean cow manure off my shoes. The weather had been sunny and warm for the past week, and the barnyard was almost dry. The black barnyard dirt turned as sticky as wet modeling clay when it rained, and only a few days ago, losing a boot in the mud was a very real possibility. And I had plenty of experience with losing my boots in the mud. It had happened to me several times.

Over the pine trees by the end of the hayfield, the sun was round and red and hung low in the sky. "Red at night, sailors' delight," is what my mother said when the sun was red as it began to set. Mom's uncles, my grandmother's brothers, had been merchant seamen who sailed out of ports in Norway.

When I reached the lane, I lifted the post, dragged the gate around, and struggled to put the top loop of wire over the post. Dad kept the loops of wire tight so the gates wouldn't sag, but the tight wires also made it harder for me to open and close the gates.

"One down, one to go," I muttered.

After what seemed like a long time but was probably only a minute, I succeeded in removing the loop of wire from the top of the gate by the pole shed. As I pulled the gate open and laid it against the fence, I thought I heard a muffled shout from inside the barn. I stood still and listened, but the only sound, besides the milker pump, was the twittering of the barn swallows as they flew over the hayfield, looking for bugs. Their lively chatter sounded like they were laughing at a joke that only barn swallows would understand.

In a minute or two, I concluded what had sounded like a yell had been my imagination, and I headed back across the barnyard.

Now that the gates had been switched, we would only have to carry the last bucket of milk to the milkhouse, rinse the milkers, turn the cows out, scrape the barn aisle, sweep the mangers, and we would be finished for the day. I was hoping by the time I reached the barn, Dad would be taking the milker off the last cow. Or maybe he would be carrying the last bucket of milk to the milkhouse. Or he might even be rinsing the milker buckets.

As it turned out, my father wasn't doing any of those things.

I walked into the barn and saw him leaning on the half door at the other end of the center aisle, clutching his shoulder.

I hurried toward him, sidestepping one of the milkers in the middle of the floor, tipped over, surrounded by a puddle of milk.

"Daddy, what happened?"

"She went crazy," Dad said, nodding toward a large, black Holstein.

The cow hopped from foot to foot. Her tail whipped back and forth and made a dull thudding sound each time it struck the steel support post next to her.

Dad straightened up and held his arm in front of his body. He used his other hand to support his elbow.

"I guess I've got a big mess to clean," he said, looking toward the milker bucket tipped over on the floor.

"I'll get it," I said.

I set the bucket upright. The cover was a few feet away. The black rubber hose which connected to the vacuum line was a few feet beyond that. The four stainless steel milker cups and their black rubber inflations were in the gutter, covered with manure. Needles and the barn cats surrounded the puddle, trying their best to lap up the spilled milk.

"Don't worry about the milker cups," Dad said. "With the way she's jumping around yet, if she kicks, she might get you in the head."

"But—what happened?" I asked.

Dad's chore cap was askew. He had a streak of dirt across one cheek, and another streak of dirt on the shoulder of his blue work shirt.

"I'm not exactly sure *what* happened," he said. "I put the milker on her, and when she was almost milked out, she started kicking. Got me in the shoulder, and when I stood up, she shoved me against the other cow."

Dad took his hand from under his elbow and straightened his cap.

"And you know how cows are," he continued, "one starts pushing, and the other one pushes back."

I had seen cows do that before when they were in the barn. They would push against each other, their feet slipping and sliding on the straw bedding.

"I was trapped between them," Dad continued. "And for a while there, I was afraid they were going to break my ribs. I tried to get my elbow into the other one, to push her over, but I couldn't do it."

"How did you get out?"

"I crawled between the stanchions."

When the cows pushed against each other, only the back half of them could connect. The stanchions at the front of the stalls kept their heads and shoulders apart.

"Does it hurt really bad?" I asked.

Dad made a face as he moved his shoulder up and down.

"Hurts plenty," he said.

For the first time, I noticed the other milker sitting near the twine barrel.

"Are we done milking?"

My father pressed his lips together in a thin attempt at a smile.

"We're as done as we're going to get," he said. "Right now, I don't care if she's got some milk left in her."

"How did the milker end up out here, anyway?"

"I had to push the milker back to make some room so I could get through. She started kicking again, caught the bucket, and that was it," Dad said.

A full milker bucket was too heavy for me to lift, and yet, the cow apparently had no trouble flinging it into the aisle with one hind foot.

"Maybe you could take the bucket out to the milkhouse and scrub it with soap and hot water," Dad said. "That would be a big help."

I took the bucket to the milkhouse to wash it. I returned to the barn and rinsed out the other milker, and then I used the push broom to sweep the milk into the gutter. Needles and the cats had gotten their fill, and Dad said I might as well clean up what was left.

When I was finished with the broom, my father was ready to turn the cows out. I followed along behind him to wave my arms so the cows would back out of their stalls.

"How would you like it if I kicked you in the shoulder for no good reason?" Dad said to the black Holstein as he used his left hand to open her stanchion. My father was right handed, and I could see that opening the stanchions with his left hand was difficult for him.

The black Holstein hastily backed out of the stall and then brushed past the other cows to get outside ahead of them.

The cows still in the aisle paid no attention to her and took their time walking to the door.

As Dad went past the calf pen and stepped across the gutter channel, I noticed he was limping slightly.

"Come on, bossy-cows. Let's go," he said. "Get out of here."

The cow nearest to Dad stopped and turned her head to look at him. We called her Martha, and she was more white than black and was plump from the grass she had been eating in the pasture.

"Don't you want to go outside and get some more grass?" Dad asked. He put his left arm around her neck to urge her forward, but Martha refused to move. Instead, she turned and rubbed her ear against Dad's hip.

"What's the matter? Are your ears itchy?" my father asked. He awkwardly massaged the base of her ear with the thumb and forefinger of his left hand.

Martha tilted her head so Dad could reach her ear better.

He laughed. "Well, at least you like me, don't you."

The truth of the matter was that all of the cows liked Dad. Except for the black one, but she didn't like anybody.

My father said happy cows gave more milk than unhappy cows, so, to keep the cows happy, he spoke to them in a quiet voice. "I don't like it when someone yells at me, and I'm sure the cows don't like to be yelled at, either," he'd say. He also gave them the best feed and plenty of fresh water, and he kept their stalls clean and well bedded. And in the summer, he fogged the barn with fly spray so the cows could rest without being bothered by flies. He also kept the radio on when we were milking because he insisted the cows liked music.

Dad didn't fool me for a minute. While it stood to reason happy cows would give more milk than unhappy cows, for Dad it was more than that. He thought of the cows as his friends. The cows knew it too.

But the black Holstein was a different story all together. From the very beginning, when she arrived on the place with a group of purebred heifers Dad had bought, she didn't want a thing to do with people.

The other heifers, including the one we called Martha, had figured out right away that my father was a person they liked. Whenever he came out to the barnyard with a pail of feed for them, they eagerly followed him to the feed trough he had built. Not the black one, though. Much of the time, she stood off by herself, away from the other cows.

Dad thought maybe once he started putting the heifers in the barn and could pay more attention to her, the black Holstein would become more friendly.

But unlike the other cows, who would stand still for as long as Dad wanted to curry them, when he curried the black heifer, sometimes she lashed out with her feet and swished her tail in a bad-tempered way.

Not one to give up too quickly, my father thought her personality might improve after she had a calf. The other cows were happy to see their newborn babies and licked them vigorously, murmuring soothing noises as they worked.

But when the black Holstein's calf was born, she didn't seem to care one way or the other. Dad had dried the baby off with an old burlap feed sack, and after its legs were stronger, he had held it up by the cow to nurse. She kept trying to kick her baby, so Dad put it into the calf pen with the older calves where it would be safe.

"This isn't looking too good," my father had said after he put the calf in the pen. "I hope she's better about the milker than she's been about everything else."

She wasn't.

When my father put the milker on the black Holstein for the first time, she promptly kicked it off.

"I should have known," he said after putting the milker on her for the fourth time.

In the following days and weeks and months, Dad never knew when the black Holstein might take exception to the milker. Sometimes she would stand quietly, but at other times, she would kick up underneath her belly to pull the milker off. Dad said he couldn't believe how fast she was with her feet. One second the milker would be where it belonged, and the next second, it would be on the floor, sucking up whatever was within reach. Since the black Holstein's milk often was contaminated with straw and other debris, Dad strained it, mixed it with milk replacer and fed it to the calves.

"The calves don't really need the extra milk, but what else are we going to do with it?" he would say. "Seems like it's defeating the purpose to try to milk her and then throw the milk away."

My father always gave the black Holstein another chance, though. And then another one, because he still thought that someday she would settle down.

From what I could see, 'someday' hadn't arrived yet.

After the cows were out of the barn, I scraped the aisle and swept it while Dad retrieved the milker cups from the gutter channel, rinsed them off, put them in a bucket of hot water with disinfectant and then went out to make sure the stock tank was full.

"I can't scrape and sweep, but I can soak the milker cups and I can keep an eye on the hose," he said.

We finished the chores and went to the house. I held the door open for Dad so he wouldn't have to let go of his elbow. I offered to untie his shoes for him, but he said he could manage it himself. He sat down by the kitchen table, and with his left hand, untied the laces of his work boots. I set the boots where Dad always put them, by the steps leading upstairs.

For the first time that I could remember, my father didn't wash up after coming in from the barn. He went into the living room and carefully lowered himself onto the couch, still holding his elbow.

"Roy! What happened?" Mom asked. She was sitting in her chair by the picture window.

"Cow kicked me in the shoulder," he said.

"Which one?"

"That black Holstein."

"You should have seen the milker," I chimed in.

"The milker?" Mom asked.

Dad flinched as he tried to find a more comfortable position. "She kicked me in the shoulder, then she got me in the leg. Then she started pushing against the other cow. Of course the other one pushed back. For a while, I thought they were going to break my ribs. I had to crawl out the front by the stanchion. Had to move the milker back so I could get through. She caught it with her foot. It ended up out in the aisle."

"It was in pieces," I added. "The cover came off. So did the hose. And the milker cups."

"Spilled the milk too, I would imagine," Mom said.

Dad sighed. "Sure did."

My mother grabbed hold of her right leg and pulled it over the left one so she could sit with her legs crossed. Mom didn't have enough strength in her legs to lift one leg over the other the way most people could.

"I hate to say this because she's such a good cow," Mom said, "but maybe you should sell her."

Dad started to shrug and then winced in pain. "I don't know how 'good' she is. She gives a lot of milk. That's about all I can say for her. The milk hardly ever ends up going to the creamery."

"That's what I meant," Mom replied.

"I always knew she'd kick me sooner or later," Dad said.

My mother frowned. "Wait a minute. Don't they make some kind of a strap that you could put on her to keep her from kicking?"

Before Dad could answer, Mom spoke up again. "Never mind. She'd probably kick you while you were trying to put it on her."

"That's probably what would happen," my father agreed.

"Well," Mom said, "we don't have to decide right now, but maybe we really should think about selling her." She looked at Dad for a moment. "Do you think anything's broken?"

He carefully squeezed his shoulder and the top of his arm. "No, I don't think anything is broken. Maybe it will be better in the morning."

"Maybe," Mom said. "But I wouldn't count on it."

The next morning, while we were doing the chores, Dad discovered he still couldn't use his right hand to open or close the stanchions. Or to lift the cover off the feed box. Or to turn on the milker pump. Or to open the vacuum valve. Later on, while we were eating breakfast, he found out he couldn't reach for the butter dish with his right hand.

Over the next several days, Dad's shoulder stayed the same. He couldn't do anything that required raising his right arm, not even something as simple as pouring a cup of coffee.

"I knew there was a reason I wasn't left handed," he commented one morning when he missed and ended up pouring coffee on the stove instead of into the cup.

Dad also couldn't use his right hand to set the milker cups and other parts of the milker on top of the rack to dry after he had washed them. Or to put gas in the tractor. Or to open the door of the pickup truck.

Within a week, he shipped the black Holstein.

"Where's she going, Daddy?" I asked, as we watched a man load the cow into a cattle truck.

"To the stockyard. For slaughter."

I didn't care much for the black Holstein, but I also didn't like to think about her being killed.

"Daddy!"

My father looked at me, and his blue eyes were filled with sadness. "I know, kiddo. I've done what I can to get her to settle down, but it hasn't worked. I can't sell her for a milk cow and take the chance that she'll hurt somebody else. She's dangerous."

I knew deep in my heart that he was right. If the black Holstein wouldn't behave herself for Dad, she couldn't get along with anybody.

It took a year for my father's shoulder to heal completely, and it wasn't until the next summer that he could once again use his right hand to put gas in the tractor or open the pickup door or lift the cover off the feed box or turn on the vacuum valve or open and close the cow stanchions or set the parts of the milkers that he had washed on the rack to dry or to pour a cup of coffee or reach for the butter dish.

Dad always wondered what was wrong with the black Holstein. None of our other cows acted like that.

Good thing too.

One was bad enough.

****

~ 10 ~
Practice Makes Perfect

For most of the morning I had been busy scraping the barn aisle, sweeping, sprinkling lime, cleaning the mangers and washing the milkers so that Dad would have time to grease both tractors, the rake and the hay baler and maybe even have time to start raking some hay. After I finished in the barn, Mom had sent me out to the garden to cut lettuce and to pull radishes. When I brought the radishes and lettuce into the house, I scrubbed the radishes in the kitchen sink and put them into a bowl. Then I rinsed the lettuce and put it on a clean dishtowel to drain.

And now it was time to eat dinner.

Dad must have been hungry too. When he came in the house, he made quick work of washing his hands and face, and a few minutes later, he sat down at the table.

"Would you say the table prayer please?" Mom asked. She folded her hands and bowed her head. Dad bowed his head as well.

"By-thy-goodness-all-are-fed-we-thank-the-Lord-for-daily-bread-Amen," I said.

My mother sat with her head bowed and then looked up at me. "You *could* say it a little slower, you know."

"I suppose she *could*, but she *didn't*," Dad replied as he took a couple of radishes and passed the bowl in my direction.

"You're no help," Mom said.

Dad grinned, and when he was sure Mom wasn't looking, his right eye closed in quick wink.

After that, no one said anything for a while. We were too busy filling our plates.

I had taken only one bite when Dad asked a question that was so unexpected, I almost choked on my mouthful of macaroni and cheese.

"I need a tractor driver," he said. "Want to give it a try?"

I was too busy chewing to answer right away. Mom said it was impolite to talk with a mouthful of food.

"I've got two loads of hay down," Dad continued. "The radio says it's going to rain this evening, and we have to get it baled."

I quickly finished chewing. "Me? You want *me* to drive the big tractor?"

For almost as long as I could remember, I had been watching Dad drive the 460 Farmall. The big red and white tractor worked as hard as Dad did. Just about the only things he didn't use the tractor for was to milk cows, stack hay in the barn, or go to town to grind feed. I had ridden on the tractor with him many times and had even steered it along straight stretches of the mile's worth of road leading to our other place. But I had never driven the four-sixty to operate a piece of machinery.

"It would be a big help if you could drive the four-sixty while I stack the wagon," Dad said. "This is first crop hay, and the bales will be too heavy for you to handle. It's one thing to pull them off the wagon and put them on the elevator. It's a lot harder to stack the wagon."

Last year we'd had some exceptionally light bales of second crop, and I had loaded a couple of wagons. But bales of first crop hay, I knew, could weigh three times as much as second crop.

I looked over at my mother.

"I don't know if I like the idea. She's awfully young," Mom said, as she reached for her cup of coffee.

Dad shrugged and dabbed a radish in the pile of salt he had sprinkled on his plate. "It's a level field. All she'd have to do is keep the tractor and the baler on the windrows. I'll make the turns for her."

"Can't you wait until Ingman gets home?" Mom asked, as she set her coffee cup on the table.

My big brother was once again working the 7-to-3 shift at the creamery in town.

"It's almost ready to bale now," Dad said. "We wouldn't be able to get started until 3:30 at the earliest if I wait for Ingman. And that's if he doesn't work overtime."

From the look on her face, I could see that my mother hadn't considered the overtime factor. Ingman often worked overtime. Sometimes he even worked a double shift.

"Please Mom?" I asked. "Pretty please?"

She tapped her finger against her lips while she thought it over.

"Well," she said at last, "I guess I *would* hate to see the hay get rain on it."

Dad tried not to smile but didn't quite make it.

"I kind of figured you'd say that," he said.

He turned to me. "I've got a couple more rounds to rake. Why don't you start walking back to the field at two o'clock."

From the time Mom and I finished the dinner dishes until it was time for me to leave seemed like an eternity. In reality, it was only forty-five minutes.

At two o'clock, I headed for the lane going toward the back of the farm. A warm breeze rustled the leaves of the oak trees growing on the Bluff, and I noticed that the leaves were turned backwards so their lighter undersides were showing. Dad said when the leaves turned backwards, that meant it was going to rain soon.

From farther up on the Bluff, a bobwhite quail sang out—bob-bob-white...bob-bob-white. At the base of the Bluff, I could see a patch of sweet fern. The leaves on the low, woody bushes smelled like the spices Mom used to make sweet pickles.

As I trudged along the sandy lane, my feet kicked up puffs of dust. The cows traveled back and forth here every day to reach the pasture at the back of the farm. When I came over the small rise near the end of the lane, Dad was already lining up the tractor, baler and wagon on a windrow. I crawled through the fence, careful to hold the barbed wire down so that I wouldn't catch my pants or the back of my shirt.

After I made it through the fence, I hiked across the end of the hayfield through the pale green hay stubble, and at the exact moment I reached the windrow, Dad took the four-sixty out of gear and set the brake.

"Good timing," he said, as he climbed off the tractor. In the heat of the mid-afternoon sunshine, the engine idled quietly.

"What do I have to do?" I asked.

"If you're going to drive the tractor," Dad said, "the first thing you have to do is get up on it."

I had been climbing up and down on tractors for quite a few years. But this was first time I would get on a tractor to actually drive it.

Steering the tractor, with Dad standing beside me, perched on the fender, wasn't the same thing at all. I would be driving the tractor by myself. Well, mostly by myself. I wouldn't have to change gears. And I wouldn't have to turn it at the end of the windrow. Dad had said he would make the turns for me.

I stood for a few seconds, looking up at the four-sixty.

"What's the matter? Are you scared to drive the tractor?" Dad asked. His voice sounded surprise.

I shook my head. "No, I'm not scared."

"Didn't think you would be," Dad said.

I put my foot on the drawbar and grabbed hold of the fender. Then I pulled myself onto the platform and settled into the seat.

My father climbed up on the tractor beside me.

"All you have to do is steer along the windrow and watch the baler to make sure it catches the hay," he said. "It'll be just like steering it along the road, except that we'll be going slower. And you'll have the baler working behind you."

"What if I have to stop?"

"Push in the clutch first and then the brake," Dad said.

I had ridden on the tractor enough to know which was the clutch and which was the brake.

"I'm going to push the seat forward a little bit and then you can try it right now," Dad said, "so we're sure you can reach the pedals."

After my father pushed the seat forward, I had no trouble reaching the clutch and the brake.

"Now let's see if you're strong enough to engage the power take-off," Dad said.

The power take-off lever was to my right, next to the fender.

"Shouldn't I give it more gas first?" I asked.

Every time I had watched Dad bale hay, he set the throttle higher before starting the baler. The four-sixty was still just on idle.

"Should have thought of that myself," Dad said. "You'd kill the engine if you tried to start the power take-off now."

I moved the throttle up, and then I grasped the power take-off lever. It required some muscle, but not as much as lifting a bucket of milk. With a clatter and a roar, the baler started.

"Push the clutch in," Dad instructed. He reached over to put the tractor into gear.

"We'll just take it real slow. First gear ought to do it," he said. "Okay, go ahead and let out the clutch. But not all at once."

I had watched Dad operate the clutch many times too. Plus, I had gotten some practice on our way to the other place. Dad would let me steer the tractor on the straight-away after we left our driveway to almost the bottom of the hill. At that point, the road curved around a hill, and one of the field driveways was on the other side of the hill.

Inch by inch, I let the clutch out until eventually, the tractor started moving forward.

And just like that, I was baling hay.

Dad nudged the throttle higher until he was satisfied the tractor was at the proper speed.

"See how the windrow is in the middle of the baler right now?" he yelled above the sound of the tractor and baler.

I turned in the seat to look back at the baler, just as I had seen Dad do maybe a hundred times.

"Try to keep the tractor where it is so the windrow stays in the middle," he said. "But if you go a little crooked and miss some hay, don't worry about it. I'll get off and pick it up the next time around."

Dad got off the tractor, took a few steps back, waited for the wagon to come by, and scrambled up on it.

"Ka-thump, ka-thump, ka-thump, ka-thump-ka-thump—ka-chinka-chinka-trip. Ka-thump, ka-thump, ka-thump, ka-thump-ka-thump—ka-chinka-chinka-trip" went the baler.

Keeping my left hand on the steering wheel, I turned in the seat so I could watch the windrow. The red paint on the fender beside me was worn off in the spot where Dad always put his hand while he was driving the tractor and watching a piece of machinery. I wanted to put my hand there, too, but I would have to lean sideways to do it, and then I wouldn't be able to watch the baler very well.

I looked back at Dad. He had already stacked two bales of hay, and as he walked forward to take the third bale out of the chute, he nodded, as if to tell me everything was going fine.

When I glanced back the next time, Dad had stacked four more bales. He walked to the front of the wagon and kicked at the pile of hay chaff that had sifted out of the chute. The wind grabbed the chaff, and a cloud of hay dust floated in front of the wagon before sinking to the ground. I knew it was important to scatter the chaff. If you didn't, then the wagon became slippery.

A short while later, we approached the end of the first windrow.

Dad pulled one bale out of the chute and set it on the wagon, then he reached far down into the chute to pull out the next bale. We were only a few feet from the end of the windrow when he hopped off the wagon, sprinted for the tractor and climbed up beside me.

"After the last of the hay goes into the baler, shut down the power take-off," he instructed.

I waited for a few seconds, then I pushed the lever down. The clattering and ka-thumping stopped.

Dad took hold of the steering wheel and turned the tractor. We drove along the end of windrows to the other side of the field, then he turned the tractor onto the last windrow.

"Get ready to start the baler," Dad said, as he straightened out the tractor.

"Okay, now."

I reached for the lever and pulled it back. With a clatter and roar, the baler started again.

Dad climbed off the tractor, stepped back, waited for the wagon to pull even, hopped up and stacked the two bales he had left sitting near the chute.

We made six trips up and down the field, and then the wagon was full. Each time we came to the end of a windrow, Dad would jump off the wagon, sprint for the tractor, climb on, make the turn, line up the baler on the next windrow, and then he would go back to the wagon.

After he had stacked the last bale, he climbed on the tractor again.

"I'll drive it down to the other end so we can pick up the empty wagon," he said. "If you'll push in the clutch, I'll take it out of gear, and then we can switch places."

Moments later, I was sitting on the fender and Dad was sitting on the tractor seat. He looked over at me, grinned, lifted the cap off his head to reposition it, and then we were on our way.

Dad stopped the tractor when we arrived at the other end of the hayfield. I got off and went back to the wagon to pull the pin, and as Dad drove forward, the tongue of the wagon dropped to the ground.

My father drove ahead of the other wagon and began backing up. I lifted the tongue, and as the baler came closer, I leaned forward so the tongue was a few inches lower. Dad tapped the throttle until the tractor was barely moving, and when the holes on the tongue and the hole in the bar on the baler that pulled the wagon were lined up, I dropped the pin in. It was one of those tasks that required a quick hand. The pin settled into the holes—'chink.'

Dad took the tractor out of gear, climbed off, came around to the back of the baler and opened the twine compartment. "I think we've got enough for the next load too," he said, "so that's good."

Inside the twine compartment was a jug of lemonade. As Dad took the jug out, the ice cubes inside rattled.

"Want a drink?" he asked, holding the jug toward me.

Drinking lemonade in the field was one of the advantages of baling hay, I had discovered. I gulped a half a dozen swallows and handed the jug back to Dad.

Circles of sweat darkened Dad's shirt underneath each of his arms. The afternoon sun felt hot on the top of my head, and I could smell the strong tea-like scent of freshly baled hay. To the west, a smudge of gray clouds had appeared on the horizon.

"There's our rain coming," Dad said as he gazed at the line of blue-gray clouds. "We'll have enough time, though, I think, to get the other load baled and to get the hay and the machinery back to the pole shed."

A few minutes later, we started to bale the second load. And once again, each time we reached the end of a windrow, Dad hopped off the wagon, sprinted for the tractor, made the turn and then jumped back on the wagon.

When we finished the last windrow, the wagon was almost full.

"Boy, now that's a good job done!" Dad said as he pulled himself up on the tractor. "I'll drive home, and we'll just go right into the pole

shed with the tractor, baler and the wagon. Then I'll come back and get
the Super C and the other wagon."

The Super C Farmall he had used to rake hay this afternoon was
parked by the fence at this end of the field.

To the west, blue-gray clouds covered one-fourth of the sky.

Dad put the tractor into gear, and soon we were driving along the
dirt road next to the Bluff. A short while later just as we went past the
barn, Ingman arrived home from work. As he got out of the car and
walked toward us, I could see that my big brother was wearing white
pants and a white tee-shirt, although I wasn't surprised because that's
what he always wore when he worked at the creamery.

My father pushed in the clutch and throttled down the engine.

Ingman grinned, showing his very white and very even teeth.

"You've got a load done already!" he exclaimed.

"Well, actually, we've got both loads done," Dad said.

Ingman's grin faltered. "Both loads?"

"That's right. We've got two loads baled. Thanks to my tractor
driver here," Dad said.

"Wait a minute," Ingman said. "You mean to tell me that my *baby
sister* drove the tractor?"

Whenever I went somewhere with Ingman, to a store or to a
restaurant, and we met someone I didn't know, he would say, "this is
my *baby* sister." As if I could forget he is twenty-one years older than
me, although Mom said other people wouldn't know that and might
think we were father and daughter, rather than big brother and little
sister.

"She sure did drive the tractor," Dad said. "For both loads. And she
didn't miss a wisp of hay."

"I can't hardly believe it," Ingman said. "My *baby sister* drove the
tractor."

"Made it a whole lot easier too," Dad said.

All afternoon, I had watched my father hop off the wagon at the end
of a windrow, sprint for the tractor and then, after he had made the turn,
climb back on the wagon. To me, it had seemed like a tremendous
amount of running back and forth.

But not nearly as much running back and forth, I suddenly realized, as he would have done otherwise.

Before this, when my father was ready to bale hay but Ingman wasn't home to help, he would drive down the windrow, let a few bales fall on the wagon, stop the tractor, stack the hay, then he would get back on the tractor, let a few more fall on the wagon, stop the tractor, stack the hay—over and over and over—until he had finished the load.

No wonder Dad was so good at running back and forth between the tractor and the wagon when it came time to make the turns at the end of a windrow.

He'd already had years of practice.

****

~ 11 ~
A Dream Come True

Mom and Dad were riding in the front seat of our car, and Loretta and I were in the back seat. It was a lovely June afternoon. A Sunday. The kind of day that if colored pictures were put into dictionaries and you looked up June, this is what you'd see—a deep blue sky with puffy white clouds, sparkling sunshine, and tall green grass waving in the breeze.

And yet, as we drove along the country road, I still couldn't quite believe it.

We were on our way to the pony farm.

For as far back as I could remember, I had wanted a pony.

Whenever we had a turkey for Thanksgiving or Christmas and my mother asked if I would like to make a wish with the wishbone, I'd wish for a pony.

Every time someone asked me what I wanted for my birthday or for Christmas, I always answered, "a pony."

On every birthday, each year with one more candle to strengthen the wish—I wished for a pony.

If Mom and I accidentally said the same thing at the same time (such as, "pass the butter, please") and then we said the rhyme: "Needles, Pins, Triplets, Twins; What goes up the chimney? Smoke; Your wish and my wish shall never be broke"—

You guessed it. I wished for a pony.

Unfortunately, each time I mentioned the subject, my mother always answered the same way. "You're too young to have a pony."

"Why am I too young? How old is old enough?" I'd ask.

"You know I'm afraid of horses," my mother would reply.

"Why are you afraid?"

"I don't know—because they're so big. I was always afraid of the workhorses when I was a little girl."

"Did the workhorses ever hurt you?"

"No. But when we put hay up in the barn, someone had to drive the team to pull the hay fork. And that was my job. And I was always terrified. Everybody else was on one side of the barn, and there I was on the other side, all by myself with those great big things."

"But the workhorses never hurt you."

"No," Mom would say. "I was just afraid of them."

"Workhorses are a whole lot bigger than a pony, you know. So why can't I have a pony?"

"Because you're too young."

"How old is old enough?"

"I don't know. But you're not old enough now, that's for sure..."

Dad, on the other hand, thought it was a fine idea. "A pony would sort of be like having Pete and Ole around again, although I guess it would be a lot smaller than Pete and Ole," he'd said when I had asked for his opinion.

Pete and Ole were the last team of workhorses my father had owned, and I could tell by the way he talked about them that he still missed them. He would tell me about the time when he worked at the canning factory and had loaned Pete and Ole to some neighbors who lived a few miles away and how the horses had come home by themselves, in the middle of the night, but had stayed hidden behind the barn, and no one knew they were back until the next day when Loretta and Ingman got home from school.

And he would tell me about the way Pete and Ole would be so glad to see him when he came home from the canning factory, following him around like puppies and nudging his arm with their noses and knocking his cap off, but that when he was ready to do some farm work, they would pretend they didn't want to be caught.

The horses had been gone from our farm for quite a few years by the time I was born, and I envied my brother and sister. They had grown up with Pete and Ole and used to ride them when they were kids.

Then, a month ago, after I had asked if I could have a pony for what must have been the thousandth time, right out of the blue, Mom said 'yes.'

Well, she didn't exactly say 'yes.'

What she really said is, "I suppose I'm never going to have any peace about it, am I, if I keep saying no."

"But," she had added, "we're going to wait until after school is out for a while. And if I hear one more word about it before then—the deal is off."

The tone of her voice and the look in her eye convinced me that she meant it, so I made sure I held up my end of the bargain, even though it just about killed me.

And that's why I had trouble believing we were on our way to the pony farm right now. Was it only this morning after we had gotten home from church that Mom had casually asked, "Would you like to go to the pony farm this afternoon?"

The people who owned the farm were known in the area for the show ponies they raised, but they had ordinary ponies too. The farm was about twenty miles away, and after we'd gone only a few miles, I felt as if we had been driving for hours.

When I had begun to think we were never going to reach our destination, my father applied the brake and put on the turn signal.

"This is it," he announced as he turned into the driveway.

The pony farm looked precisely the way I had imagined. Big white farmhouse. A stable. Lots of corrals. And ponies everywhere.

I was still staring out the window when Loretta leaned over and touched my shoulder.

"Aren't you going to get out?" she said.

I turned to look at her. "What?"

"Aren't you going to get out of the car?"

Oh, yes. Get out of the car.

How could I look at ponies if I didn't get out of the car?

"Don't buy one that's wild," Mom cautioned from the front seat.

Although my mother had finally given her permission, she didn't especially like the idea of getting a pony.

Dad paused before shutting the car door and looked in at my mother. "Now, Ma," he said, "do you *really* think I'd let her get one that's wild?"

My mother smiled sheepishly. "No, I guess not."

Dad, Loretta and I were going to look at ponies, but because of the polio paralysis, Mom had decided she would stay in the car. Walking around with crutches was hard enough, but trying to maneuver on unfamiliar ground was harder yet, she said.

I had no more than gotten out of the car when I heard the screen door slam shut.

"Can I help you?" asked a man who was settling a cap on his head as he came down the porch steps.

Actually, it wasn't a cap. Dad wore caps. This was a hat. A *cowboy* hat. A *straw* cowboy hat.

"We're looking for a pony," Dad explained. "It's for her." He tipped his head in my direction.

"We've got lots of nice ponies," the man said.

"We don't want anything fancy," Dad continued. "Just something she can ride around on for fun."

The man smiled in a way that told me he knew everything there was to know about ponies and about riding ponies.

"We have plenty of nice ponies we don't take to the horse shows for one reason or another," he said.

The man started with the corral next to the barn. From there we moved to a corral on other side of the barn. And from there we moved into the barn itself—a long, low building with an aisle running down the middle and stalls on both sides.

During the next hour and a half, we looked at many ponies.

Mares and geldings.

Larger ones.

Smaller ones.

Black ones.

White ones.

Brown ones.

But with each pony the man brought out, Dad found something wrong with it. This one had a stubborn look, he said, and he didn't like the way that one stomped its back foot when he patted its hind quarters. The next one laid its ears back when Dad walked up from the front. The one after that stood with its front feet turned in toward each other. And the one after *that* stood with its feet turned out.

Then there was the pretty gray pony with a black mane and tail.

In Dad's opinion, the gray pony was too old. The man said it was twelve and that twelve wasn't old for a pony. I knew from reading in the 'H' volume of our encyclopedia set, which had been perused so often it automatically fell open to the horse entry, that each year in a horse's life is equal to three human years. That meant the gray pony was like a thirty-six-year-old person. And I didn't think thirty-six sounded old. After all, Dad was *lots* older than thirty-six, and HE didn't seem 'old.' But Dad still said something a few years younger would be better.

The next pony, a palomino that was a golden color just a shade darker than our dog, Needles, was only three. But in Dad's opinion, three was too young.

"We want one who knows a little bit about life," Dad explained.

The man put the pony back into its stall and latched the door.

"I'm sorry," he said, "but that's all I've got to show you."

What was he talking about? With so many ponies around here, how could that be the last one?

"Nothing else you think would work?" Dad asked.

The man shook his head. "The rest of what we've got are either stallions, pregnant mares, or mares with a nursing foal. I know you wouldn't want a stallion, although if you wanted a pregnant mare, or a mare and foal, I'd be happy to show them to you."

"No," Dad said, "one pony is all we need. My wife isn't too happy about getting one, so I'm sure we couldn't talk her into two."

The man grinned. "I see."

"Well," Dad said, turning to go out of the stable, "if you don't have anything else to show us, thanks for your time."

My stomach suddenly felt hollow.

After all the years I had spent wishing.

After finally convincing Mom to give her permission.

After spending the whole afternoon looking at ponies…

This was IT?

My throat began to tighten up, and I knew that in a minute, I would probably start crying. And I didn't want to cry. Not in front of the nice man.

Loretta put her arm around me. "Don't worry," she said. "We'll find a pony. Not today, I guess. But someday."

Someday?

I hated it when Mom said 'someday' because that usually meant 'never.' Like when I asked if we were ever going to go on a summer vacation—a few of the other kids at school went on summer vacations with their families but we were too busy milking cows and baling hay to do anything like that—and she said, "I don't know...maybe *someday*."

We had almost reached the door of the stable when the man cleared his throat. "Wait! I forgot about one."

I spun around to look at him.

"She's in the far pasture," he continued. "We tried breeding her this year, but something went wrong."

I hastily wiped the tears from my eyes.

"I can show her to you if you want. Do you have time?" the man asked.

Dad pulled out his pocket watch. He glanced at me. "Yes," he said. "We've got time."

We waited in the shade of the barn while the man went out to the pasture. He came back ten minutes later leading a plump, brown pony with light brown spots and a white mane and tail—and I knew that this was THE ONE.

Now all I had to do was convince my father.

"How old is she?" Dad asked.

"Let's see," the man said, as he latched the pasture gate behind them. "She's...five. No. Six. She just had a birthday."

"That's a good age," Dad said. "Not too old and not too young. And you say you tried breeding her?"

The man turned from the gate and patted the pony's neck. "Yes. And we thought she was going to have a foal, too, but then we found out she wasn't. Or maybe she was and lost it early on. We just don't know."

"I see," Dad said, walking all the way around the plump pony who in turn was watching Dad.

"Want me to lead her around for you? While your little girl rides?" the man asked.

"No, I'll lead her around," Dad replied. "That way I can see if we're going to get along."

The man handed Dad the lead rope.

I petted the pony's soft, brown nose. She nuzzled my shirt and left a streak of muddy dirt on my shoulder.

"How come your nose is so dirty, little pony?" Loretta said.

The pony turned toward my big sister. She looked at Loretta and then took a step closer and nuzzled my sister's bare arm.

"Eeeeeek," Loretta said. "Your whiskers are prickly."

Dad and the man smiled, but they laughed out loud when the pony began licking my sister's arm.

"She sure seems like a friendly little thing," Dad commented.

"You can say that again," Loretta said, wiping off her arm with a Kleenex she had taken from her purse.

Dad lifted me onto the pony's back.

If I had been sure before that this was 'the one' only by looking at her, I was completely convinced now. The pony felt just right. Not too tall and not too short.

Dad took hold of the pony's halter. "Come on, girl," he said.

He led the pony along the driveway. "Is it fun?" he asked, looking over his shoulder at me.

Fun? This was more than just 'fun.' It was Heaven. It was all the Christmases that had ever been, or ever would be, rolled together into a single moment.

"Oh, Daddy! Please? Please-please-please-please-pleeeeease can we get this one?"

"Hmmmm...maybe," Dad said. "Let's see how the trip back to the barn goes."

He let go of the pony's halter. Although he was now holding the end of the lead rope, when he turned around, the pony turned around too, and as Dad walked along the driveway, the pony walked quietly beside him.

After we arrived at the spot where Loretta and the man were standing, Dad stopped. So did the pony. He patted her neck. "Good girl," he said. "Good horse."

"Why did you do that, Dad?" I asked.

"Do what?"

"Why did you let go of her halter?"

My father tossed the end of the lead rope over his shoulder—as if this was something he had done many times before—so that both his hands were free.

"Some horses, when they get the opportunity, will try to run back to the barn," he said. "I wanted to see what she'd do."

"I get it," Loretta said. "It was a test. Did she pass?"

"I don't know? Did she?" he asked, giving me a sideways look.

"Oh, yes. She's a very good pony," I said.

Dad took a step forward. "I want to try a couple more things."

He put his arm around the pony's neck, and she leaned her head against him and rubbed her ear against his ribs.

Dad removed his arm and slid his hand under the pony's thick, white foretop. She tilted her head to the side, as if she were really enjoying the attention.

"You can tell a lot about a horse by putting your arm around its neck," he explained as he rubbed the pony's ears.

This time she turned her head in the other direction, so Dad could get at her ears better.

"If they let you put your arm around 'em," he continued, "it means they like people…and you don't want one that won't let you touch its ears…so…yes…I think this one will work out fine."

It took a few seconds for Dad's words to sink in.

"Do you mean it? We can get this one?" I asked, wondering if I had heard him say what I thought he had said.

My father smiled. "Yes, we can get this one. If this is the one you want."

I slipped off the pony's back and walked around to her head.

"Do you want to be my pony?" I asked.

The little brown pony lifted her nose and nuzzled my hair. Then she licked my forehead. Once. Twice. Three times. Unlike the cows' sandpapery tongues, the pony's tongue was smooth.

Dad, Loretta and the man from the pony farm all burst out laughing.

"I think that means she'd like to be your pony," the man said.

I threw my arms around her neck. "I want you to be my pony too."

But as I rested my cheek against her thick white mane, it dawned on me that—in a way—this was the end of a dream come true.

Although even better yet, it was also just the beginning.

****

Going Home

Dad reached into the front pocket of his shirt. My father always carried his billfold buttoned into the front pocket. Even today when he was wearing a short-sleeved light green shirt, instead of his usual blue work shirt, the billfold was in his front pocket. If a shirt didn't have a pocket, Dad wouldn't wear it.

"What do I owe you," he said to the man from the pony farm.

The man turned toward the brown pony with the white mane and tail. "Sixty-five dollars," he said.

My father opened his billfold. "Sixty-five it is. My wife said we shouldn't go over seventy-five, so she'll be happy about that."

He pulled out three twenty-dollar bills and a five and handed the money to the man, who folded it and put it in his pants pocket.

A little while later, we left the pony farm and headed for home. The entire trip passed in a blur, but I had better things to think about than the scenery, anyway, because now that I had my very own pony, what was I going to name her?

I considered many possibilities. Snickers (because chocolate is brown and Mom and I both loved Snickers candy bars). Marshmallow (because of the white mane and tail). Katrina (only because I liked the name). Rose (another named I liked). Hazel (because she was the color of hazel nuts). Ginger (more yellowish than the pony but I thought it was a nice name). And finally—Spot (an awful name, but I was getting desperate, and the pony *was* covered with spots, although Dad said the spots were called 'dapples.')

Mom and Dad suggested other names. Trigger, for one, which Dad thought sounded like a good name until Mom pointed out it would be better for a boy horse and this was a girl. And then there was Nancy, which Mom suggested. "I've always liked the name Nancy," Mom said. And Petunia, another name from Dad. When I asked why he thought Petunia sounded like a good name, he said the pony looked like the type who would eat her way through a bed of petunias. Then Mom suggested Florie.

"Florie was a black mare my dad owned," she said.

I reminded my mother that the pony was brown and not black.

"I only thought of Florie because Pa's Florie was nice," Mom said.

My eyebrows inched upward. This was first time I had heard my mother even so much as hint that a horse might be nice.

"Florie was a sweet old girl, but Pa got mad at her because she was lazy," Mom continued. "And then there was the time he *really* got mad at her when he was plowing one spring. Later on he felt bad about it, though."

"What happened?" I asked.

Mom twisted around in the front seat so she could see me better. "All morning long Pa was plowing the little field back by where the pines are now. It was a nice day, so we had the window open in the kitchen, and we could hear him yelling 'Get up, Florie! Get up, Florie!' When it was almost time for dinner, I packed some food and took it back to him. By the time I got there, he'd already unhitched the horses. He always did that when he stopped to eat so they could rest in the shade."

"But why did Grandpa Nils feel bad?" I asked. Even though my grandfather had died many years before I was born, I had seen pictures of him and could imagine him plowing the little field by the pines.

"Pa and I sat in the shade so he could eat his dinner. The next thing we knew, Florie laid down and—guess what?"

"What?" I said.

"She had a baby."

I blinked a couple of times. "She did what?"

"Gave birth to her foal. Pa knew she was supposed to be due in several weeks. He had no idea she was so close. If he had known that, he never would have hitched her to the plow. Here the poor thing had been pulling a plow all morning long and she was in labor. He never quite forgave himself for that one."

"What did Grandpa Nils do then? Did he make Florie plow again?"

Mom shook her head. "Oh, no. We waited until the colt could stand up and walk, and then we took them back to the barn." She smiled. "Pa felt so bad that he gave Florie some extra oats, even though she didn't need it because she was fat already. Then he spent a long time brushing her."

Loretta and I were once again riding in the back seat together, as we had on the way to the pony farm, and after Mom finished telling us about Florie, my sister turned to look at me.

"I just had an idea," Loretta said. "What do you think of the name Dusty? She has all those dapples on her—like somebody dusted her with a powder puff."

Now that she mentioned it, that's exactly what the pony looked like.

"Don't you think Dusty would be a good name, Dad?" Loretta asked.

"Seems perfect."

"I think Dusty's a good name too," Mom said.

Right after Dad told the man we were going to buy the pony, my father had led her over to the car so my mother could get a good look at her. The pony had stuck her head into the open window, and Mom had let out a little shriek, although she allowed herself a faint smile when Dad pulled the pony back and she had started licking Dad's arm.

"Why—she's kind of like a big dog, isn't she," my mother had said.

Since Mom, Dad and Loretta thought Dusty was a good name for the pony, I decided to try it out.

"Giddy-up Dusty," I said.

"Whoa, Dusty."

"Here Dusty."

"Is that going to work?" Dad asked.

"Dusty is a very good name," I said. "But she needs a second name too."

"A second name?" Loretta asked.

"Like mine is Rae."

"Oh," Mom said. "You mean a middle name. What about Marie?"

"Dusty Marie..."

Nope.

"Lou?" Loretta suggested.

"Dusty Lou?"

I shook my head.

"Road," Dad said.

"Road?" I inquired. "What kind of a name is that?"

"Then she'd be," Dad said, glancing into the rearview mirror, "Dusty Road."

"Dad-deeeee!"

My father grinned.

"How about," Loretta said, "Ann."

"Dusty Ann?"

"That's part of your name, too," Mom said.

Giving the pony part of my name was a *wonderful* idea.

"Okay," I said, "her real name is Dusty Ann but we'll only call her Dusty for short."

"Dusty it is," Mom agreed.

"Dad? When are we going to bring Dusty home?"

My father didn't answer right away, but instead rolled down his window a little more. "Let's see...we can't go tomorrow. We'll be baling hay. And if the weather holds, we'll be baling all week. Then there'll be second crop hay, and oats to combine after that." He paused, as if gathering his thoughts. "Maybe sometime after school starts."

After school started? But that was all the way at the end of the summer...

"Roy," Mom said, "you shouldn't tease her like that."

Dad glanced into the rearview mirror again, and he was wearing his 'cat that swallowed the canary' smile. "I guess that just leaves tonight after milking, then, doesn't it."

I could hardly believe my ears. Tonight! After milking!

"Oh, Daddy! Could we?"

"It's as good a time as any. Like I said, we're going to be busy with the haying this week and next week, too, and I don't see any sense in waiting two weeks before we haul her home."

A few minutes later, Dad turned onto the road leading to our farm. As soon as he parked the car in the driveway, I got out and ran for the house. I rushed up the steps, yanked open the screen door, and when I plunged into the kitchen, I saw my brother sitting at the table with the latest edition of *Hoard's Dairyman* open in front of him.

"Guess what?" I said breathlessly, throwing myself into a chair.

"What?" Ingman said.

"You'll just *never* guess."

"Ummm, let's see," Ingman replied, frowning. "I think I remember hearing you were going to the pony farm this afternoon, so I bet you found...a cow!"

I shook my head.

"A mule?"

"Uh-uh."

"I give up then."

"We found a pony."

My brother's blue eyes widened and his jaw dropped. "A pony? No. I don't believe it. You couldn't have found a pony. Could you?"

I nodded happily.

"Is it a girl pony or a boy pony?" he asked.

"A girl. And her name is Dusty."

"Dusty? She must need a bath."

"No. She's got spots."

"Spots?"

"She's brown and she's got lighter spots all over. Dad said they're called dapples. Loretta said it looked like somebody dusted her with a powder puff."

While I told Ingman about my pony, Mom, Dad and Loretta came into the house. I turned around in my chair so I could see the clock. The big hand was on the eleven and the little hand was on the five. It was nearly five o'clock. Dad started milking around 6:30, and the chores took an hour and half to finish, so that meant we wouldn't be going to get Dusty for another three hours yet.

"Daddy, how come we can't get Dusty right now?" I asked.

My father had sat down in a kitchen chair and was changing into his work shoes. "You know why we can't go right now—because we've got to do the chores."

"Are you going to start milking early?"

Dad pulled out his pocket watch. "Probably not, it's already five."

"But then...that means...we won't leave until eight o'clock!"

In the meantime, my brother had gotten up to pour a cold glass of milk. Ingman put the pitcher back in the refrigerator and took a long swallow from his glass.

"You know," he said, setting the half-empty glass on the table, "if you want to go get that pony right after we eat supper, I can milk the cows by myself."

I stared at my big brother. "Ingman? Would you?"

He smiled. "Yes, I think I can manage it alone—for once."

"Daddy! Can we?"

Before Dad could answer, Ingman spoke up again. "I think it would be better if you went earlier so you can get home before dark. If you're only driving someplace, that's one thing. But if you're hauling a pony…"

My father finished lacing up his work boot. "You're right. I suppose it *would* be better to go when we're done with supper."

The day before, Loretta had made a big bowl of macaroni and tuna salad, so after Dad and Ingman had put the cows in the barn and fed them, we ate a quick supper of salad and coldcut sandwiches. While Ingman went to the barn to start the milking, Dad and I got into our old, battered, dark-green pickup, which had tall wooden sides around the bed of the truck.

Once again, the trip to the pony farm seemed like an awfully long way, but finally we arrived. The man we had talked to earlier told Dad to back the truck up to the ditch by the driveway so the bed was level with the lawn. Then he went to the barn to get Dusty. Instead of turning the pony out into the pasture, he had put her into a stall. The man led the pony to the truck, and she walked right in, as if she'd been doing it every day of her life.

"Think you'll be able to get her out?" the man asked.

"Sure," Dad said, as he tied the rope in a square knot. "We've got a bank just like this at home."

And in fact, we did. On the side of the lawn by the driveway, the yard dropped off to form a bank several feet high.

"I suppose we'd better be going. Before she gets nervous just standing there," Dad said, offering his hand to the man.

The man shook hands with Dad, then he looked at me. "Have fun with your pony. And take good care of her."

"I will. I promise!" I said.

The man nodded and smiled. As we climbed into the truck, he lifted one hand to wave before heading toward the house.

Dad started the pickup and eased away from the bank. He pulled out of the driveway, and a short while later, turned onto a back road.

"Why are we taking this road? And how come we're not going very fast, Daddy?" I asked, wondering if there was something wrong with our old pickup truck. I didn't know much about trucks, but even I could tell this one wasn't going to last much longer. The body was rusting out in places, and sometimes it didn't want to start.

"I'd rather take the back roads. It's hard for horses to stand up when you're hauling them, so we don't want to drive fast," my father replied, carefully pushing in the clutch so he could shift to a higher gear. "We wouldn't want her to get off balance and fall down and hurt herself."

It was a cool, clear evening, and here and there, herds of dairy cattle grazed peacefully in pastures along the road. Some of the cows were Guernseys, some were Holsteins, and Dad said the darker brown ones were Brown Swiss.

All of a sudden, Dusty let out a long, loud whinny. I turned toward the back window. The pony stood with her chin resting on the tall side of the truck, gazing into the distance.

"Why did she do that?" I asked.

Dad shrugged. "Don't know. Maybe she just felt like it. All horses whinny once in a while."

"You don't think she's scared, do you?"

Dad peered into the rearview mirror. "No, I don't think she's scared. She looks happy enough."

A little while later, Dusty whinnied again.

And again.

And then again.

"Why is she *doing* that?" I asked.

My father took a quick look out of the side window. "Oh," he said, "I bet it's the cows. She's talking to the cows."

"Daddy! Ponies can't talk!"

Once when I had asked Dad why our Guernsey cow, Number, would let me ride on her back but the other cows wouldn't, he said she'd told him she liked kids who pretended they were cowboys. I had informed him that cows couldn't talk, and Dad had agreed but said they could still let you know what they were thinking.

"Ponies can't talk the way we do, but they can talk in their own way," my father replied.

While I thought about what he'd said, once again, Dusty whinnied.

"Well, if she's talking to the cows—what's she saying then?"

Dad gave me a sidelong glance. "Can't you figure it out?"

I shook my head.

"She's saying 'look at meee-eee—I'm going hoooooome.'"

I giggled. "That's funny, Daddy."

When we pulled into the yard, it was almost sunset. One of the things I enjoyed most about summer was the long evenings of daylight.

My father parked by the bank in front of the house, opened the tailgate and untied Dusty. Putting each foot down slowly and carefully, she backed out of the truck. After all four feet were on the ground, she started to eat the thick green grass growing in the lawn.

Dad smiled as he closed the tailgate. "Looks like she's right to home already. Sometimes horses get upset when they're in a new place. But I don't think she's nervous."

No, Dusty didn't look at all nervous.

While we were unloading Dusty, my sister and mother had come from the house, and then several minutes later, Ingman came from the barn. He had let the cows out, and a few of them were leaving the barnyard, headed for the pasture south of the driveway.

As more of the herd entered the pasture, Dusty stopped picking grass and stood with her head held high, staring at the cows. In the twinkling of an eye, the pony drew a deep breath and whinnied so loud that the effort shook her whole body from nose to tail. The cows stopped and turned to look in the direction of the front yard.

My mother inched backward, her slate-blue eyes wide with alarm. "What's wrong with her, Roy?"

"Nothing," Dad said, turning to wink at me. "She's just letting the cows know she's home."

Mom frowned. "Letting the cows know...?"

Dad explained how Dusty had whinnied every time she saw a herd of cattle on our way back from the pony farm. "Sounded just like she was saying, "look at meeeeee. I'm going hooooooome!" he said.

"Why would she whinny at cows?" Mom asked.

Dad shrugged his shoulders. "I don't know. Your guess is as good as mine."

Ingman patted the pony's rump. "She sure is a cute little thing."

"Isn't she, though," Loretta said.

Dusty watched the cows for a while longer. Then she went back to picking grass.

"What are you going to do with her for tonight?" Mom asked.

Dad gathered up the lead rope. "We're going to put her in the barn in that empty calf pen," he said. "Then tomorrow, she can explore her new pasture. I know just the spot for her, right behind the house."

My father turned to me. "Wanna ride your pony to the barn?"

"Could I?"

"That's what a pony is for, isn't it?" he said as he lifted me onto Dusty's back.

Dad tugged on the lead rope, and the pony stopped grazing and fell into step beside him. When we reached the driveway, her hooves went clip-clop, clip-clop, clip-clop, and to me, it was the sweetest sound in the whole world.

Dusty was really and truly home—once and for all.

****

~ 13 ~
A Different Sort of Cow

When the cattle truck backed up to the barn one cloudy summer afternoon, I hurried outside to watch. We'd never had a Jersey before, so after I learned that Dad had bought one at an auction, I didn't know what to expect.

The day had started out sunny, but by dinnertime, the sky had clouded over, and now the air felt damp, as if maybe it would rain soon. Because of the humidity, I could smell the barnyard, even from where I stood in front of the barn watching the cattle truck. Whenever the air was humid, the odor of cow manure carried a long way.

The man driving the truck climbed down from the cab, went around to the back and pulled out the ramp so the end of it was inside the barn door.

"One Jersey and two Holsteins—right?" the man asked. He was a few inches shorter than Dad and had broad shoulders and thick forearms. His reddish-blond hair matched the color of his sunburned face, and he wore it in a crew-cut so short, for a few seconds after he got out of the truck, I thought he was bald.

"That's what I bought," Dad said, "one Jersey and two Holsteins."

The man grinned. "I like to check *before* I unload 'em. One time when I'd already unloaded the cows, it turned out I was at the wrong place. Cows didn't want to go back in the truck neither."

Dad nodded and scratched his chin. "I can see how that would be. I suppose they figured they'd already made enough trips for one day."

The man walked up the ramp and threw open the doors in the back. "Come on, girls. You're home."

He walked back down the ramp. "I like to give 'em a chance to see if they wanna come out on their own. Usually they don't, though."

After a minute when no cows appeared in the door of the truck, the man sighed, went back up the ramp, and disappeared inside. For a little while, everything was quiet. Then came the sound of scrambling hooves followed by a couple of loud thuds and a muffled "OWWW! You stepped on my foot!"

Moments later, a black and white face appeared in the doorway.

"You're this far," we heard the man say, "now just take a couple more steps."

I looked up into the truck. The man was directly behind the cow, pushing on her rump for all he was worth. The cow had planted her front feet and didn't appear to be interested in going any farther.

"Hold on a minute," Dad said. He went into the barn, and when he returned, he was carrying a bucket of the ground corn and oats and molasses that we fed the cows.

"You'd better stand back," he said to me. "If she comes out of there in a hurry, I wouldn't want you to get run over."

I took a couple of steps backward. Getting run over by a cow didn't sound too appealing.

"Come-bossy," Dad said, shaking the bucket, "look what I've got."

While Dad continued to shake the bucket invitingly, the man pushed on the cow's rump. The Holstein took one hesitant step and then another and another, and then, without warning, she leaped down the ramp and disappeared into the barn.

My father jumped back to get out of her way.

"I suppose we'd better see where she went to," he said.

Inside the barn, the Holstein trotted down the middle of the aisle. Clickety-clack, clickety-clack went her feet as they struck the concrete floor. Upon reaching the other end of the barn, she stopped and turned to look at us.

"Come-bossy, come-bossy," Dad said in a soothing voice. He slowly walked toward her.

When he was almost to the other end of the barn, the Holstein, desperate for an escape route, hopped over the gutter channel and trotted down the cement in front of the stations.

"Shoot. I didn't want her to do that," Dad said. He hurried back the way he had come, trying to cut her off before she reached the door.

The Holstein took one look at Dad, and with great difficulty, turned around in the narrow space between the stanchions and the barn wall. Her hind legs connected with a watering cup—which I tended to think of as upside down army helmets mounted next to each stanchion—and knocked it to the floor. The crash of the metal cup spurred her forward.

"Didn't want her to do that, either," Dad said, as the cow galloped toward the opposite end of the barn.

"Quick," he said. "Run down there and stand by the gutter on the other side so she doesn't go up that way."

I slipped between the stanchions and ran as fast I could. I made it just in time. The Holstein was about to leap over the gutter channel, but when she saw me, she slid to a stop, her feet skidding on the cement floor.

A loud clattering sounded from the other end of the barn, and then the second Holstein came trotting down the barn aisle.

"Great," Dad muttered. "Now we've got two of 'em to deal with."

The cattle truck driver appeared in the barn. "Sorry. I didn't think she was going to do that. I put the gate across the door so the Jersey'll stay in there until we're ready for her."

The two Holsteins met in the middle of the barn aisle and stood shoulder to shoulder. When one moved a few steps, the other moved with her.

As my father walked toward the two cows, they backed away and then took off in opposite directions. The cattle truck driver waved his arms to keep one of them from running over him. She made an abrupt ninety-degree turn into a stall.

"I think we've got her now," the truck driver said gleefully.

"Don't be too sure," Dad replied.

My father was right.

The truck driver took a step in the Holstein's direction, and she sailed over the stall divider, like the horses I had seen pictured in the encyclopedia going over jumps, cleared the gutter channel and trotted down the center aisle to the other end of the barn, her companion right behind her.

In the end, it took us a half an hour to get the two Holsteins into stanchions, and by the time we were finished, another watering cup had been knocked to the floor and three piles of cow manure had been deposited in the manger, along with a large pool of cow urine.

"This isn't exactly where I wanted them, but it's good enough for the time being," Dad said, as he pulled a red bandanna handkerchief out of his back pocket and dabbed at the trickles of sweat running down the side of his face.

The cattle truck driver was perspiring too. Beads of sweat had popped out on his forehead.

"Okay. Now we can get the Jersey," the driver said. He went into the truck, and a minute later, a small butterscotch colored cow carefully picked her way down the ramp. She stepped into the barn and stopped.

"Come-bossy," Dad said, shaking the feed pail.

The Jersey's head snapped around. She stared at Dad and then hurried toward him. He started to say something, but before he could get the words out, she had already stuck her nose in the pail.

My father laughed. "You must be hungry," he said.

He pulled the feed pail away from her nose and stepped over the gutter channel into a cow stall. The Jersey stayed right on his heels.

Dad squeezed through the open stanchion and dumped the rest of the feed in the manger. The Jersey followed, put her head into the stanchion, and seconds later, while the cow chewed a mouthful of feed, Dad closed the stanchion.

"Well," he said, "at least that one was easy."

"Some difference," said the cattle truck driver. He had been standing near the door ever since the Jersey came into the barn.

Dad turned to me. "If you'll take him to the house, Ma can write out a check. I'll stay here and keep on eye on the cows."

A short while later, with a check in his pocket, the cattle truck driver got into his truck and left. The sky was darker than it was before I had gone into the house, and I felt a raindrop hit the top of my head while another splashed my bare arm. I didn't waste any time getting into the barn.

"I think the Holsteins are starting to settle down. I hope so anyway," Dad said. He had replaced one watering cup and was working on the other.

The two Holsteins glanced around nervously, but they weren't swishing their tails or stomping their feet. A pile of feed sat in front of each of them, although they hadn't touched it yet.

I studied the Jersey, who was standing quietly in her stall, head down, licking up the last of the feed Dad had given her.

"She's so little," I said.

Most of our cows were Holsteins although we also had a couple of Guernseys. If I stood next to the Holsteins, I could not see over their backs. The Guernseys were smaller than the Holsteins, but the Jersey, by comparison, was downright tiny.

"Can I pet her?" I asked.

"If you want to," Dad replied. "I don't think she'll mind."

My father had put the Jersey into the first stall in the barn next to the feed box. She stopped licking the manger and turned her head to look at me. She had large brown eyes, and her nose, the area around her forehead and her ears were dark brown. She was the prettiest little cow I had ever seen. In many ways, she reminded me of the white-tail deer that came out into the alfalfa field behind the barn just around sunset. I turned my attention to her front legs.

"Look at how small her feet are!" I exclaimed.

Dad came up beside me. "She's awfully delicate, all the way around," he said. As he patted the cow's back, I reached out to pat her shoulder.

One of the reasons why I liked the Guernseys in our herd is that they were so calm. Unlike the Holsteins, nothing seemed to bother the Guernseys much. I accidentally dropped a calf pail after I had fed the calves yesterday, but the Guernsey next to the calf pen, a cow we called Reddy because she was a solid dark red all over from nose to tail, never moved a muscle.

"Will she be like Reddy?" I wondered.

"What do mean, 'like Reddy?'"

"When I dropped the calf pail yesterday, she didn't even notice," I said.

My father smiled. Reddy was one of his favorite cows. "I don't know if she'll be like Reddy," he said. "I guess we'll have to wait and see what she's like after you drop another calf pail."

I looked at Dad, and he grinned.

Dad walked around on the other side of the cow, stood there for a few seconds, and then walked back.

"Maybe you should give Jersey two more scoops of feed," he said.

"Jersey?" I said.

"She's the only Jersey in the herd, so I figure Jersey would be a good name for her."

"Two *more* scoops?" I said.

Each of the cows received two scoops of ground feed morning and evening; those that milked a little heavier received an extra scoop. None of our cows had ever gotten *two* extra scoops.

Dad ran his hand over Jersey's flank. "I think we should give her four every time we feed. I don't want her to lose any weight. They tell me she's a heavy milker, and from the looks of her, I believe it."

Jersey—now that Dad had pointed it out—was not exactly skin and bones, but she was thinner than our other cows.

Seeing as the petite fawn-colored cow with the big brown eyes was in the end stall next to the feed box, all I had to do was reach over to give her more.

I scooped up some feed and turned around. Jersey was watching me eagerly and straining forward in her stanchion. She waited until I dumped the feed, and then she dug into it, as if she hadn't seen anything to eat for a month, even though she had just finished eating the two scoops Dad had given her. As I dumped the second scoop, she never even paused but continued to sweep feed into her mouth with her rough tongue.

Dad shook his head. "Boy, she's got a good appetite."

All of our cows liked their feed, but I had to admit I'd never seen one eat with this much enthusiasm.

I turned and tossed the scoop back into the feed box.

At least I *meant* to toss it into the feed box. The metal scoop hit the side of the wooden box and then clattered on the cement floor.

Faster than you could snap your fingers, the two Holsteins jumped backward in their stanchions. As the feed scoop rolled from side to side on the concrete floor, they snorted, stomped their feet and twisted their heads this way and that, trying to escape what they perceived as an obviously dangerous situation.

"Here now," Dad said, "don't hurt yourselves. I'd rather not have any more swelled up knees."

A while back a barn cat had jumped up in the window and frightened one of our Holsteins. The cow slipped and banged her knee on the concrete lip to which the stanchions were anchored. The cow's knee had swelled to twice its normal size, and she was lame for several weeks after that.

I leaned down to retrieve the feed scoop, and when I straightened up, I noticed that Jersey was still eating and not paying any attention to all of the commotion going on in the barn.

Dad noticed too.

"Jersey," he said, "you're quite the cow."

I carefully set the scoop inside the feed box. "Why did you buy a Jersey, anyway, Dad?"

My father lifted off his cap and settled it more firmly on his head. "Thought it might be fun," he replied. "I've always heard they were a little bit different from other cows."

A *little* different?

From what I could see, the small butterscotch-colored cow happily licking up the last of her feed while the two Holsteins—who had not yet touched their feed and were still fidgeting and glancing around nervously as if they expected another feed scoop to come crashing out of nowhere—wasn't a 'little bit' different.

She was in a category all her own.

****

~ 14 ~
Needles Has a Picnic

D ad had left for town two hours ago, so I knew he ought to be coming home soon with our brand new picnic table. I found a spot in the shade of the silver maple tree in the front yard and sat on the ground. From here, I could see the truck as soon as it came over the first hill by the church.

Some of my friends at school talked about going on picnics where they cooked hamburgers in a park and then sat at a picnic table to eat. But we never went on picnics. Dad was too busy with the farm work, and besides, Mom couldn't get around well enough because of the polio to spend an afternoon in a park.

Once we had a picnic table, though, we could have picnics right in our very own backyard and could eat supper under the trees in the shade where it was cooler. Eating supper in the kitchen when it was ninety degrees outside and the sun had moved around to the west and was shining directly into the kitchen window was like eating inside of a pressure cooker. That's what Dad said. And I figured he ought to know, seeing as he used to work in the pressure cooker room at a canning factory.

The leaves of the silver maple above me rustled in the breeze, and from the patch of white clover a few feet away, I could hear honey bees buzzing as they flew from flower to flower.

I had only been sitting under the maple tree a few minutes when one of the barn cats arrived to keep me company. Needles was lying in the shade closer to the tree trunk, but he faced the road and wasn't paying any attention to me. If my father left in the truck but didn't take Needles with him, the dog would stay in the front yard until Dad returned.

I petted the tabby cat's head, tracing my fingers along the stripes between her ears. The cat began to purr, and after a while she climbed into my lap, turned around in a circle and settled down. The purring slowed and almost stopped as she closed her eyes and fell asleep.

My foot had started to prickle with pins and needles, and I was wondering if I would be able to change my position without waking the cat, when I saw the truck.

"Dad's here!" I said.

In an instant, the cat woke up. She stepped off my lap onto the grass and stretched and arched her back, while Needles rose to his feet, his tail wagging from side to side.

By the time some of the feeling had returned to my foot, Dad was coming up the driveway. As he drove past us, I could see not one, but two cable spools in the back of the truck. Last night at supper, Loretta had announced that the electric company she worked for had some cable spools to give away and that maybe we could get one to use as a picnic table.

I had asked what a cable spool was, and Dad had explained that the spools were used for holding electrical cable and were made of wood and looked somewhat like the wooden spools that held the thread my sister used when she made clothes for herself or for me or for Mom, except the thread spools were much smaller, of course.

While Dad parked near the garage, the cat, Needles and I hurried across the yard and headed for the truck.

"Hi Daddy!"

"All three of ya were waitin' for me, huh?" Dad said. He leaned over to pet the cat.

Needles, not to be outdone by another animal on the place, pushed the cat aside and stepped forward to receive his fair share of attention from Dad.

"How come you got two?" I wondered.

My father gave the cat and the dog a final pat on the head.

"The big one's going to be the top, and the smaller one will be the bottom," he said.

Dad took off his cap and smoothed back his hair. "If we use only the biggest spool, we'll have problems with our chairs. We won't be able to pull them close to the table."

"Why not?"

"The bottom would stick out too far. The chair legs would be sitting on it, and then we'd be tilted backwards," Dad explained.

Even though we would now have a picnic table, we would have to carry chairs from the house when we wanted to have a picnic. Last night, Mom had said she would enjoy eating outside, but when Dad said he could build some benches, Mom said she would feel more comfortable sitting in a chair.

"How are you going to get them out of the truck?" I asked.

"Just like we got Dusty out of the truck after we brought her home," Dad replied.

The edge of the lawn formed a bank shallower near the top of the driveway and much steeper where the driveway headed downhill. The night we had brought my pony home, Dad had backed up to the bank so the bed of the truck was even with the lawn. Dusty had walked out of the truck as nice as you please.

My father opened the driver's side door, and Needles jumped in ahead of him.

"I'm only going to back the truck around," Dad said to Needles. "It won't be much of a ride."

The dog flopped down on the seat with a happy sigh.

"Never mind," Dad said as he got behind the steering wheel.

After he was satisfied that the pickup was where he wanted it, my father shut off the engine and opened the door. Needles scrambled over Dad's lap and hopped to the ground. He watched with bright eyes and ears perked as Dad opened the tailgate and squeezed past the spools. The biggest of the two spools was nearly as high as Dad's shoulders.

My father grabbed hold of the smallest cable spool, rolled it to the edge of the tailgate and then out onto the lawn. It took him a little bit longer to unload the other one.

After the second spool was safely resting on the grass, Dad removed his cap and pulled a blue bandanna handkerchief out of his back pocket to wipe the sweat off his face. "Kind of warm today, isn't it," he said, as he stuffed the handkerchief back into his pocket.

In my opinion, 'warm' was an understatement. It was hot. Now that I was out in the sun, I wished I were sitting in the shade again. Today was one of those summer days when it felt like you were trying to breathe through a warm, wet, wool blanket.

"What are you going to do with the spools now?" I asked.

"It's a ways to go, but if you'll help me, we're going to move them to the machine shed," Dad replied.

My father pushed on one side of the biggest spool and I pushed on the other. Rolling the cable spool was like rolling a tire, except that I couldn't see over the top of the spool. As we started across the lawn, Needles pranced along beside us.

We passed the kitchen window where my mother stood by the sink, watching. She waved. Dad nodded, and I took one hand off the spool and twiddled my fingers in return.

After we had gone back for the second spool, which wasn't nearly so hard to roll, my father went into the shed for a hammer and some nails, and in what seemed like only a few minutes, he had removed the top part of the big spool and had nailed it to the smaller spool. Then, between the two of us, we managed to move our new picnic table into the shade of the silver maples at the back of the lawn.

"This'll be a nice place to eat, won't it," Dad said.

He turned and looked around the yard. "Just think of it," he continued. "At suppertime, it'll be shady here, and we'll be able to feel the breeze and hear the birds singing and—"

"And you won't have to use your handkerchief," I said.

On sweltering days when we ate supper in the kitchen, Dad kept reaching for the bandanna handkerchief to mop the sweat off his face.

Dad grinned and touched the back pocket where he kept his handkerchief. "Nope. I won't have to use my hankie. At least I hope not."

In the evening, we got ready to eat our very first picnic supper. Loretta said she planned to paint the picnic table this weekend but that she didn't see any reason why we couldn't put a tablecloth on it for tonight. Mom searched through the drawer where she kept her tablecloths and found a red-and-white checkered one I had never seen before.

"How come we don't use that tablecloth?" I asked.

My mother shrugged as she pushed the drawer shut. "We never go on picnics."

A few minutes later, the red-and-white tablecloth had been spread out on the picnic table.

As my big sister and I carried plates, utensils and chairs outside, Needles followed us from the house to the picnic table and back to the house again. I could tell from the expression on the dog's face that he wasn't exactly sure what we were doing but thought he should keep an eye on us—just in case it turned out to be important.

Later on, when Loretta and I carried the food outside, Needles *knew* that paying attention was a good idea. He trotted along next to us, nose in the air, snuffling when he caught the scent of the hamburgers.

As I followed my sister across the yard toward the picnic table, I took a firmer grip on the tin tray. Mom kept a set of tin trays in the storage space under the steps leading upstairs that we called the pantry, but I had never seen the trays used for anything. The trays were decorated with pictures of pine cones and pine needles. Carrying the tray made me feel like one of the waiters I had seen on television, and I hoped I wouldn't trip over my own feet. I would never live it down if I ended up dumping our supper on the grass.

Loretta and I put the food on the picnic table while Mom descended the porch steps and started across the lawn. Her crutches made a clicking noise as she moved one foot forward and then the other, one foot forward and then the other.

"Do you think we should tie the dog up?" Mom asked when she arrived at the picnic table. She grasped the back of a chair and laid her crutches on the ground beside it.

Needles sat a few feet away. From time to time, he put his nose into the air and sniffed. When we ate supper in the house, he laid underneath the table by Dad's feet. Needles was an inside-outside dog, which meant that when Dad was in the house, he was in the house, and that when Dad went outside, he went outside. The only time Needles did not want to go outside was during a thunderstorm. I knew just how Needles felt. I didn't want to go outside, either, when it stormed.

My father turned to look at the dog. "I think he'll be all right. He doesn't bother us while we're eating in the house."

That first picnic supper was every bit as good as I thought it would be. Hamburgers (my favorite). Potato salad (also one of my favorites). And strawberry shortcake for dessert with whipped cream (my extra-special favorite).

"Isn't this lovely?" Loretta asked, spreading mustard on top of the ketchup she had already put on her hamburger.

"This *is* nice," Dad agreed.

"Much cooler than it is in the kitchen," Mom added.

"I just wish Ingman was here," I said.

For the past few days, my big brother had been working the 3-to-11 shift at the creamery. He wouldn't come home tonight until long after I had fallen asleep.

"We'll have more picnics this summer, so Ingman will get to have picnics too," Loretta said.

"I think the only one who's not quite sure what to make of this is Needles," Dad said.

Since the dog couldn't occupy his customary spot under the table, he sat next to Dad. A few minutes later he moved around to sit on the other side of my father. A few minutes after that, he sat down next to me.

By the time we were eating dessert, Needles had moved to my mother's side of the table where he was lying with his nose on his paws.

"What are you doing over here?" Mom said, looking at Needles.

"Maybe he's hoping you'll give him those hamburgers," Dad said.

Two hamburgers were left on the plate sitting next to Mom's glass of lemonade.

My mother looked across the table at Dad. "Are you out of your mind? Give the dog perfectly good hamburger?"

"Don't get upset. I'm only teasing," Dad said.

"Hmmmphhh!" Mom said. "Why would I give him hamburger? I don't even like dogs."

My mother said she only tolerated Needles going in and out of the house because he was a family pet, although whether she truly did not like dogs was a question I had not yet been able to answer. The only thing I knew for sure was that during a thunderstorm, Needles stayed close to Mom until the storm was over, sometimes even going so far as to put himself between my mother and the kitchen cupboard while she was washing the dishes.

"Well," Dad said as he pushed back his plate after he had finished his strawberry shortcake, "I guess it's time to milk the cows."

My father stood up and headed for the barn. Needles got to his feet and trotted along at Dad's heels.

As soon as Dad and Needles left to do the chores, Mom started back across the yard, and Loretta and I began carrying the chairs inside. Loretta took a chair in each hand, but I could only carry one, which left one chair by the picnic table.

After we put the chairs back where they belonged around the kitchen table, Loretta filled the sink with hot water and added a couple of squirts of dish soap.

"If I fill the sink now, when we come back with the dishes, we can put them in to soak right away," she said.

"Good idea," said Mom, who had only just arrived in the kitchen. It always took my mother a long time to cover a short distance.

A few minutes later on our return trip to the picnic table, I immediately noticed something was missing.

"What happened to the hamburgers?" I asked.

Instead of two hamburgers, there was nothing but an empty plate.

A very *clean* empty plate.

The potato salad bowl—which still had a little bit left in it before we carried the chairs inside—looked suspiciously clean too.

And there was Needles, sitting behind the table, licking his chops.

"Needles," Loretta said, shaking her finger at him. "I thought you went to the barn with Dad."

The dog looked up at her and began to pant. His pink tongue slipped from between his front teeth, and for just a second, I could have almost sworn he was grinning.

"Oh, so *that's* where you are," said a voice from behind us.

Loretta and I turned to see Dad walking across the lawn.

"After I put the milkers together, I realized Needles wasn't in the barn like he usually is at chore time. I kinda figured he might come back out here."

"Look at the plates, Daddy!" I said.

My father frowned when he saw the plate where the hamburgers had been. "I thought there were two…" His voice trailed off. "Needles! You didn't eat both of those hamburgers did you?"

The dog slunk around the table and sat by Dad's feet.

"And look at the potato salad bowl," Loretta said.

"And the shortcake plates," I added.

"You did a good job of washing those dishes, Needles," Dad said.

The image of the Cocker Spaniel-Spitz dog with floppy ears and short legs getting up on the chair and then standing on the picnic table so he could lick the plates brought a grin to my face.

"That's a good one, Daddy! Needles washed the dishes!"

"You can laugh if you want to," Loretta said, "but I don't know what we're going to tell Mother."

My father thought about it for a few seconds.

"Tell her Needles wanted to have a picnic too," he said.

When we brought the dishes in the house and told Mom what had happened, she took it much better than we thought she would.

"Hmmmm…I guess it was our own fault for leaving the food out there," she said. "I suppose Needles is wishing we'd have picnic suppers every day."

Needles wasn't the only one. I wished we could have picnic suppers every day too. Even if it did take twice as long to set the table. And to clear away the dishes.

Because now that we had finally gotten started, we had an awful lot of picnics to make up for.

****

~ 15 ~
Popsicle Blues

From underneath the maple tree in front of the house came the sound of the lawn mower. The living room windows were open, and as I crawled into the closet in the hallway near the bathroom, I could smell freshly cut grass.

It was a Saturday afternoon, and for the last half an hour, my big sister had been mowing the lawn. I would rather be outside, too, but Mom had asked me to help her look for a certain pair of shoes she wanted to wear to church tomorrow. Because of the polio paralysis, my mother couldn't get into the back of the closet, so it was my job to remove the boxes and other items while Mom sat on a chair nearby.

We had found the shoes, a pair of beige flats, and all but one box had been put back in the closet, when the lawn mower stopped. A minute later, Loretta came into the house. She wore a sleeveless white blouse and a pair of sky-blue shorts. A blue headband held her dark curly hair back from her forehead. Her legs were speckled with chopped up bits of green grass, and on her feet, she was wearing white tennis shoes smeared with grass stains.

"I didn't realize it was so hot outside," she said, as she took a glass from the cupboard and turned on the tap at the kitchen sink.

Loretta was nineteen years old when Mom found out I was on the way, so my sister had quit her job in the Twin Cities to move home and help with the housework. Before I was born, the doctors were convinced that because of my mother's physical condition, neither of us would survive. They were wrong, of course.

The year after I was born, my big sister began working as an assistant bookkeeper at the electric cooperative that supplied electricity to our farm and to many of the rural areas in our county. On Saturday mornings, she cleaned the house and washed clothes, and on Saturday afternoons during the summer, she often mowed the lawn or worked in her flower beds.

Loretta took a sip from her glass, set it on the kitchen table, and pulled out a chair to sit down.

"I suppose Dad and Ingman will want something cold to drink after baling hay all afternoon," she said.

"There's always water. And we've got plenty of that," Mom replied as she leaned on the chair she had used by the closet and pushed it back to the table.

"Well, yes," Loretta said, "but I was thinking of something besides water. It's hard work mowing the lawn, but it's even harder work baling hay."

She turned in my direction. "Would you like to go to Norton with me?" she asked. "We can take those empties back and get some more pop. Do you think Dad and Ingman would appreciate pop to drink?"

As far as I was concerned, a trip to the Norton store was the highlight of any day. The little country store was a mile and a half from our farm. At one time there were other businesses too, but all that remained was the store and a few houses. The country school where my mother and sister and brother had gone to grade school, but which was now empty and not used for anything, was just down the road from the store.

About once a week during the summer, we went to the store to buy soda pop and other snacks, such as potato chips and candy bars. Dad enjoyed eating a snack in the evening when he had finished the milking, although my father was just as likely to eat an apple or an orange or a banana or a bowl of ice cream with fresh blackberries on top, if the blackberries were ripe and we had recently picked a pail.

"I suppose if you *want* to go to Norton—but you don't have to," Mom said.

"I'm ready for a break anyway," Loretta replied. "It's too hot to mow any more right now."

My sister took the headband off, ran a brush through her hair and used a wet washcloth to wipe the grass off her legs. Instead of the white tennis shoes stained green from mowing the lawn, she slipped on a pair of sandals, and then we were ready to go. On our way out of the house, we picked up the three cartons of empty soda pop bottles that were in the porch.

It was hot outside, but it was hotter inside Loretta's sea green four-door Chevrolet Bel-Air, even though the car was parked in the shade of the silver maple by the gas barrel. We rolled down the windows, and by the time we had driven the half mile to the main road, it felt much cooler in the car. At the stop sign, we turned right, and after another mile on the state highway, we arrived at the Norton store, a long, narrow, one-story building painted white with a two-story house attached to the back.

After the brilliant sunshine outside, the interior of the store was dark and, it seemed to me, rather gloomy. The wooden floor creaked under our feet as we threaded our way through narrow aisles to reach the cartons of soda pop stacked up like the extra bags of barn lime Dad kept in the granary.

"What-cha up to today?" the store owner asked.

"I *was* mowing the lawn," Loretta said, "but it's too hot. Dad and Ingman are baling hay, so we figured we'd get some pop for them."

"Pop's always good on a hot day," the store owner replied with a smile.

"Can I have a Push-up? I mean, *may* I have a Push-up?" I asked.

Mom said it was impolite to ask by saying 'can.' "Yes, you're probably capable of doing what you're asking, but the real question is, do you have permission?" she'd say.

"If you want a Push-up, go and get one," my sister replied.

I went to the freezer case, opened the cover and reached down inside. The sides of the freezer were coated with a thick layer of frost. The Popsicles were right next to the Push-Ups, and just the thought of root beer Popsicles made my mouth water.

"What about root beer Popsicles too?" I asked.

Loretta checked her purse. "I've only got enough money for the pop and the Push-up. We'll either have to get the Popsicles and two cartons of pop, or three of pop. But not Popsicles, pop and a Push-up. Take your pick."

I thought about it for a moment. "Pop," I said.

"That it, then?" the store owner asked when we set the three cartons of soda pop on the counter.

"And this," I said, holding up the Push-Up. Orange sherbet was one of my favorites, and orange Push-Ups were the next best thing.

Loretta paid for our purchases, and we headed out to the car. The Norton store was set back only a few feet from the highway, and in the heat of the afternoon, I could smell the oil in the blacktop.

A short while later, we arrived home with the three kinds of pop we had bought. Root beer. Pepsi. And Orange Crush. And all in returnable bottles.

I grabbed the carton of root beer while Loretta carried the cartons of Pepsi and Orange Crush. I had always been fascinated by the cardboard cartons. What a great idea to make something with compartments in it to hold bottles of soda pop and a handle at the top.

"Uh-oh," Loretta said as we walked toward the house.

"What?" I asked.

"The whole point of going to Norton was to get pop so Dad and Ingman would have something cold to drink," she said. "Except that the pop isn't cold. And it won't be for a long time after we put it in the refrigerator. Not for a few hours."

I opened the porch door, and the answer to our dilemma stood right in front of me. Inside the porch was the chest freezer Mom and Dad had just bought. Dad was planning to build a freezer room in the machine shed, but until then, the freezer had been installed in the porch.

"I know!" I said. "We can put the pop in the freezer."

Mom, who I could see through the open kitchen door, sat by the table with a glass of water and the newspaper. She looked up over her reading glasses.

"Put the pop in the freezer?" she said. "Why?"

"So it'll get cold faster," I explained.

"I don't think we should," Mom said. "What if we forget about it?"

"What if we forget about it!" I said. "Who could forget a thing like that?"

I knew I wasn't going to forget we had soda pop. The empties had been sitting on the porch for almost a week, and I was starting to wonder if we were ever going to get some more.

"What do you think about it, Loretta?" Mom asked.

My sister set the cartons of soda pop on the kitchen table. "I suppose we *could* put it in the freezer. Maybe for a half an hour or an hour, at the most."

Mom looked doubtful.

"But Dad and Ingman are going to be home soon," I said, "and they won't want to drink warm pop."

I didn't want to drink warm soda pop, either, for that matter.

My mother looked at the kitchen clock. "Let's see…they left right after dinner and it's three now," she said. "I suppose they'll be home in an hour, or maybe less."

"That would be okay then, wouldn't it?" Loretta said. "As soon as they get here with the hay, we'll take the pop out and put it in the refrigerator."

"Well," Mom said, "if you think it will be all right until then."

"Are we going to put all of it in the freezer?" I asked.

Loretta shook her head. "No, one is enough. The other two can go in the refrigerator."

"But if we put all three in the freezer, it will all be cold, and then they can have whatever kind they want," I said, proud of myself for coming up with the idea.

"How much pop do you think Dad and Ingman are going to drink right away?" Loretta asked.

"They might not want the same kind," I protested.

My mother held up her hand. "One is enough," she said, "the other two can go in the refrigerator."

I still thought all three should be put in the freezer, but if Mom said one was enough, that was the end of the discussion.

"Okay, so which one should go in the freezer?" Loretta asked

I didn't even have to think about it. "Root beer," I said.

"Root beer it is."

A few minutes later, Loretta changed into her white and green tennis shoes. "I'm going out to mow some more of the lawn," she said.

After Loretta had started the mower, Mom asked me to go outside and see if the clothes were dry. They were, so I took them off the clothesline and brought the basket into the house. Mom and I were almost done folding the basket of clothes when Loretta came back inside and asked me to help her move the picnic table. I hung around outside in the shade of the silver maples, waiting for her to finish that section of the yard so we could move the table back. The grass was so thick, however, that the lawn mower plugged up after only two passes underneath the trees. It took a while for Loretta to clean the mower, and by the time I went back into the house, Mom was worried.

"I wonder if something is wrong," she said.

"Wrong with what?"

"I'm thinking Dad and Ingman should've been home by now," Mom continued. "Why don't you and Loretta take the car and see what's going on."

I went outside to deliver Mom's message, and ten minutes later, Loretta and I arrived at the 'other place' about a mile north of our farm.

From the road, we could see the tractor, baler and a wagon standing in the middle of the field. Dad and Ingman were bent over the front of the baler. Half a load of hay sat behind the baler. The other wagon was full.

Loretta drove into the first field driveway and parked the car. We got out and walked across the hay stubble to where Dad and Ingman were working on the baler.

"Oooo-ouch," Loretta said. "I forgot that hay can be scratchy on the ankles."

"It *is* scratchy," I agreed. Normally, if I were going out in the hayfield, I would have put on a pair of jeans, instead of wearing shorts and tennis shoes. Fortunately for us, the baler was closer to this end of the field rather than at the far end.

Dad and Ingman looked up as we approached. They were now crouched by the big fly-wheel on the front of the baler, and they were each holding a wrench. Needles was resting in the shade of the hay wagon, keeping a close eye on Dad and Ingman.

"Boy, are we glad you're here," Dad said. "Hay's so heavy, we've been going through shear bolts one after another. Thought we had enough extra with us too."

Ingman wiped the sweat off his forehead. "Could you go home and get some more shear bolts for us?"

"Where are they?" Loretta asked.

"On the workbench in the machine shed," Dad replied, "in a small paper bag. I just bought some the other day. Should have brought 'em with us, I guess."

Fifteen minutes later, Loretta and I returned with the shear bolts.

Dad took the small paper bag from me, pulled out one of the bolts and held it up. "Funny, isn't it, that something this small is keeping us from finishing a load of hay."

"If the shear bolt will hold, once we get it changed, we'll have the load done in not too long, and then we'll be coming home," Ingman said.

"Do you want us to stay here?" Loretta asked.

"You can stay if you want to," Dad said. "We've got the tools we need. All we didn't have was the extra bolts. But if we should happen to need something else, it'll save time if you can go and get it."

So we stayed and watched while Dad and Ingman changed the shear bolt.

"We'll know within a minute or two if it'll hold," Ingman said.

Dad started the tractor, and Ingman hopped on the wagon. As Dad pulled the power take-off lever, Loretta and I moved back a few steps. The baler erupted with a clatter and a roar, and then the tractor was moving forward, following the windrow. Needles jumped up on the wagon to stand beside my big brother.

"So far so good, it looks like," Loretta said after a few minutes had gone by.

Dad made the turn at the end of the field, and then they were headed back in our direction.

"I think it's hotter out here than it is at home," my sister commented as we watched the tractor and baler moving toward us.

The sun blazed white in the light-blue sky, and there was no wind to speak of. A cloud of dust hovered over the baler.

When Dad and Ingman were three-fourths of the way back, Loretta turned toward the car.

"I don't know much about it, but the baler looks like it's working okay now," she said.

We got into the car, and as they arrived at the end of the field, Dad lifted his hand and motioned toward the road.

"I think he means we can go home," Loretta said, and with that, she started the car.

When we walked into the house a little while later, Mom was sitting in the living room by the picture window. "Is the baler working?" she asked.

On our trip home to get the shear bolts, Loretta had taken a minute to tell Mom what was going on.

"They changed the bolt and had made almost a round by the time we left," Loretta replied. "There was only that part of a load to finish."

"Good," Mom said. "Glad to hear it."

Although it didn't take long to drive over to the other place with a car or the pickup truck, it took much longer to haul a load of hay, and it was almost time for supper when Dad and Ingman came home. They parked one load by the elevator in front of the barn so they could unload it after milking. They left the other load sitting in the driveway by the machine shed.

"I can't believe how hot it was out in that hayfield today. I sure am thirsty," Dad announced as he walked into the kitchen.

Thirsty?

I looked at Loretta—and she looked at me.

"Oh, NO!" Mom said. "I *knew* we were going to forget!"

I dashed into the porch and opened the freezer.

"Jeepers," Dad said, peering over my shoulder.

Columns of frozen root beer rose straight up out of the broken bottle necks. A couple of them had the bottle caps perched on top.

"Root beer Popsicles!" I exclaimed.

"Don't even *think* about it," Mom said. "There's probably broken glass in it."

"Is that all there is?" Dad asked, sounding disappointed.

"No," Loretta said, "there's Pepsi and Orange Crush in the refrigerator."

"How long's it been in the freezer?" Ingman wondered, as he stood beside me and gazed at the broken bottles.

"Since three o'clock," Mom said.

"No wonder it's froze," Dad replied. "It's almost six now."

"I don't know about anybody else, but I need something to drink," Ingman said, going into the kitchen and heading for the refrigerator.

"Get one for me too," Dad said, following my big brother.

"What kind?" Ingman asked.

"Orange," Dad answered as he rummaged around in the utensil drawer, looking for the bottle opener. My brother set a bottle of Pepsi and a bottle of Orange Crush on the counter, and after Dad found the bottle opener, he pried off both caps. The bottle caps landed on the counter—'clink…clink.'

"Is it cold enough?" Loretta asked while Dad poured Orange Crush into a glass.

He took one swallow and then another one. "Perfect. This is just what I needed right about now."

"Meeeeee too," Ingman said.

Dad pulled three more glasses out of the cupboard. "Well? Aren't the rest of you going to have some?"

"After the kind of afternoon we've had, I think we deserve it," Mom said.

Dad scowled. "*We?*" he said. "Ingman and I baled. Loretta and the kiddo helped us fix the baler, but—"

He gave my mother a pointed look.

"I sat here and worried," Mom said. "I knew there was something wrong when you weren't back by four."

Dad winked. "That counts. We gotta have somebody to do the worrying for us."

I went to the refrigerator. "What kind?"

"Pepsi," Mom replied.

"I'll have Pepsi too," Loretta said.

Dad opened the bottle for me and poured Pepsi into the three glasses. "There you go," he said.

I had no more than taken a sip from my glass when the real tragedy of the situation hit me like the force of a hay bale falling off the elevator when the bale was almost up into the barn.

"We don't have any root beer!" I wailed. "It's all ruined!"

Loretta set her glass on the table. "Well, yes," she said, "you're right about that. It *is* ruined."

"Can't be helped now," Dad said.

Ingman glanced at Mom. "We could thaw it out," he offered with a sly grin.

"No we can't," my mother said, "it's probably got glass in it."

"Good thing we didn't put all of it in the freezer," Loretta said.

I wasn't about to admit it, but for once, I was glad Mom and Loretta hadn't listened to me.

Maybe we should have gotten those root beer Popsicles, after all.

****

~ 16 ~
On Top of the World

I set the empty five-gallon pail on the ground beside my father. "Will you fill this for Dusty?" I asked. On hot summer days, my plump brown pony often drank two pails of water.

Dad stood by the barnyard fence, keeping an eye on the hose as it ran into the stock tank. From the point where the short sleeves of his blue chambray work shirt ended to the tips of his fingers, his arms were tanned as dark as the fudge my sister made for Christmas. Dad's cap was pulled low on his forehead to shade his eyes from the summer sun. Needles sat next to his feet. No matter what my father was doing, the furry Cocker Spaniel mix with the bushy skirts was sure to be somewhere close by.

The last time I had been in the house, the thin red line in the thermometer by the kitchen window said it was eighty-five degrees. For most of the afternoon, our dairy cows had been standing in the shade at the bottom of the wooded hill behind the barn.

The cows had come up to the barnyard only a few minutes ago. Every now and then, one of them would lift her front foot to chase the flies away from her belly while she was drinking, and her knee would bang against the metal stock tank.

In answer to my request, Dad put the hose in the pail, and when the pail was full, he put the hose back into the tank.

"She's not here," he said, leaning to one side so he could get a better look at the cows.

"What?" I asked as I picked up the bucket of fresh water for Dusty. "Who's not here?"

"The one that I figured was getting pretty close this morning," Dad replied.

I set the bucket down again and turned toward the barnyard.

Sure enough, the young Holstein who had grown much bigger in the belly over the past few months was not with the herd.

"When are we going to look for her, Daddy?"

"Right now," my father said. "Just as soon as you give Dusty her pail of water. We're gonna take the truck, though. It's too hot to carry a calf all the way back to the barn."

Eighty-five degrees wasn't the hottest it had been this summer, but it was humid today, and I was glad we were taking the truck to look for the cow and her calf. After walking out to Dusty's pasture to get her pail, I could feel sweat prickling between my shoulder blades. Once we found them, the calf would be placed in the back of the truck. Many times I had sat on the tailgate by the calf while Dad drove slowly so the cow could keep up.

As I took the pail of water to Dusty, Dad started the truck and drove it through the barnyard and into the lane. On several occasions during the past few weeks, when I checked the pony's water, I discovered she had tipped her bucket over. Dad said spilling a full bucket was like a game for her and that I should tie it to the fence post with a piece of twine string.

After I was satisfied the pail was tied securely, I headed toward the truck. Needles trotted in front of me, his feathery tail thrashing from side to side. He had followed me past the corncrib to the gate leading into Dusty's pasture, and while I tied the twine string, he had taken a good, long drink. The hose had been running into the tank for quite some time, so the water was as cold as melting snow in early spring.

I opened the truck door, and Needles leaped in ahead of me and hopped on the seat. This was exactly the kind of adventure he enjoyed. Not only were we going to look for a cow and a calf, but we were also taking the pickup truck. And as far as Needles was concerned, any excuse to ride in the truck was good enough for him.

"Are ya ready to see if we can find that cow, Needles?" Dad asked as I closed the door and settled back against the seat. He reached over and patted the dog's head.

Needles yawned, opening his jaws wide and then snapping them together, the way he did when he could hardly contain himself.

Dad liked to have the dog come with us when we were looking for a cow and a calf, because if the cow was hiding in a patch of brush where we couldn't see her, Needles would find her for us. Either that or the cow would find Needles. More than once, he had been chased under the pickup truck or under the fence by a cow who thought he was too close to her baby.

Although the cows could have their calves in many different places around the farm, two spots turned out to be the most popular. One was a shallow wooded ravine that Dad called 'the Hole.' A small spring ran through one side of the ravine and the ground was spongy and soft and covered with a thick layer of green moss. The other place was a ten-acre woods at the back of the farm where there was also a spring. When anyone in our family referred to 'the Spring,' that meant the woods at the back of the farm. Mom said during the dry years of the Great Depression, she had carried a shovel back to the Spring so she could dig out an area where the cows could drink.

Dad pushed in the clutch, and soon we were bouncing along the road next to the Bluff. From inside the glove compartment came the jingling of wrenches and screwdrivers. My father always kept a few wrenches and screwdrivers in the glove compartment because he said a person never knew when he might need one or the other.

As we drove along, I looked up at the Bluff. It was by far the biggest hill on our farm, and it blocked the view of the northwestern horizon behind the barn. At the very top was the quarry where my great-grandfather had dug out the stone to build the basement of our house.

Needles sat upright on the seat between us, quivering with excitement. Even his ears were quivering. He stood up, put his paws on the dash, stared out the windshield and then sat down again.

Dad looked at the dog and grinned. "You're like a little kid who just can't sit still, aren't ya puppy," he said.

An hour later when we drove past the Bluff again, Needles was no longer quivering with excitement. He was lying on the seat, panting so hard that saliva dripped off the end of his lolling tongue.

I could understand why Needles felt that way. Sweat trickled down my back, and the welts on my neck from the mosquitoes we had stirred up when we walked through the woods by the Spring were starting to itch.

Dad parked the truck in the shade by the machine shed, and after I opened the door, Needles dragged himself out and slowly walked to

Dusty's pail so he could get a drink. When he was finished, he stretched out flat on the grass in the shade of the granary, heaved a big sigh and closed his eyes.

My father smiled. "Needles will sleep good tonight, I think."

"Where have you been?" Ingman asked as Dad and I walked into the kitchen a few minutes later.

My big brother had arrived home from the creamery while we were out with the truck.

"We were looking for that cow I figured was getting close," Dad said. He hung his sweat-stained cap on the newel post and went to the sink to get a glass of water. My throat felt as if I had swallowed a cotton ball, so I could hardly wait to get a drink of water too.

"I take it that means you didn't find her," Ingman said.

Dad shook his head as he lifted the glass to his lips.

"Where did you look?" my brother asked.

"Everywhere," Dad replied when he had finished swallowing, "except at the top of the Bluff of course."

Blackberry brambles, sweet fern, jack pine and other brush grew among the trees around the bottom of the Bluff, and from time to time, a cow gave birth to her calf there, but the cows never had their calves farther up the hill—it was much too steep.

"Did you check the Hole?" Ingman asked.

"First place we looked," Dad said.

With my father in the lead, Dad, Needles and I had threaded our way past patches of box elder and prickly ash, until at last, we had reached the bottom of the wooded ravine.

But there was no cow or calf to be seen anywhere.

"What about the Spring?" Ingman inquired.

I turned on the faucet to fill my glass again. "That was the next place we looked," I said.

Right around the spring that flowed out of the hillside and down to the fence line were oak trees and patches of brush. Wild grapevine as big around as my wrist rose out of the ground to climb the trunks of the some of trees. Dad, Needles and I had walked from one end of the woods to the other. But we didn't see a cow and calf there, either.

"Well, what about the bottom of the Bluff?" Ingman wondered.

"Nope," Dad said. "We walked all the way around until we got back to the truck again."

The east and north sides of the Bluff were thick with blackberry brambles, and as we made our way around, we had seen all kinds of green berries covering the briars. Dad said that as long as we didn't get a hail storm, we would have plenty of ripe blackberries to pick in another month or so.

What we didn't see, however, was a cow and a calf.

"Are we going to look for her again tonight after chores?" I asked.

My father turned on the tap again and filled his glass half full. "We've been all over the farm. I don't know where else to look. We must have missed her somehow."

"Maybe not," Ingman said.

"What's that?" Dad asked.

"Maybe you didn't miss her. Maybe she's at the top of the Bluff."

My father set his empty glass on the counter. "I'd be surprised if she's up there."

"I think I'll take a look anyway, just to make sure," Ingman said.

"Suit yourself," Dad replied.

A few hours later, while Dad and I milked, Ingman set out for the hill behind the barn.

When my brother returned, his arms were scratched and bleeding— but he was grinning triumphantly.

"She's up there all right," Ingman said, leaning against the barnyard fence while he caught his breath. "Right up on top by the quarry."

"You've got to be kidding," Dad said.

We had finished milking a little while ago, and once again, my father was waiting for the stock tank to fill. Dad looked at the sun poised over the western horizon. "If we hurry," he said, "we should be able to get them down before dark."

The grin vanished from Ingman's face. "I'm afraid it won't be quite that easy."

"Why not?" Dad said.

My big brother reached for the hose to drink from it.

"That calf is as wild as a little deer," he explained after he had put the hose back in the stock tank. "She can run faster than just about anything I've ever seen. At least, I think it's a she. Not that I could get close enough to tell for sure."

Dad rubbed the back of his neck. "Great," he muttered. "Should have figured as much. Baby's had all day to get her legs working."

Ingman's grin returned. "I'll say her legs are working."

As Dad and Ingman talked, I saw something black and white moving through the trees at the bottom of the Bluff.

"Look," I said, pointing. "There she is."

My father and brother turned.

"Well, I'll be," Dad said, "she's bringing the calf down herself."

"Wouldn't you know it," Ingman muttered, "after I scratch myself all to pieces trying to find them."

"Guess that's the way it goes sometimes," Dad said.

"Guess so," Ingman agreed.

But while we stood there watching, it became obvious the cow was alone. She walked into the barnyard, where the other cows stood around in small groups.

Dad turned toward the barn. "Why don't we put her inside so she can eat her feed and drink some water, and while she's doing that, let's see if we can't get that calf."

"Can I go too, Daddy?" I asked.

My father shook his head. "It's too steep and too rough up there."

I was about to protest that I was perfectly capable of climbing the Bluff when Dad spoke up again.

"Besides," he said, "I need someone to keep an eye on the hose."

The stock tank was two-thirds full, but before the cows went out to pasture for the night, they would drink from the tank.

My father and brother headed for the top of the Bluff, and I waited by the barnyard fence, watching the tank while it filled and swatting at the mosquitoes that kept trying to bite my arms.

After spending so much time with Dad looking for the cow and calf, and after my brother's report that the calf was "as wild as little deer," I could scarcely wait to see what the baby looked like. Needles waited with me. He had started to follow along, but when Dad told him to stay, he had willingly returned and sat down by my feet. Apparently Needles had had enough of traipsing through the brush for one day.

A short time later, Dad and Ingman came out from the trees at the bottom of the Bluff. But no little calf trotted between them.

And not only that, but as they approached the barnyard, I could see one half of the front of Dad's blue shirt hanging in ribbons.

I walked across the barnyard to meet them.

"What happened to your shirt, Daddy?" I asked.

My father's expression was grim. "Blackberries," he said.

"Blackberries?"

"Right at the top of the Bluff, there's an open spot, and it's filled with the biggest blackberry briars I've ever seen," Ingman said.

"Canes are as big around as my thumb," Dad grumbled.

And so it went.

Over the next week, Dad and Ingman made many trips to the top of the Bluff. But each time, they returned without the calf.

Because the baby needed its mother's milk, Dad let the cow come and go as she pleased. Every morning and evening, she traveled down to the barn to eat some feed and to get a drink of water. And then she went back to take care of her calf.

After the first week of trying to catch the calf, my father and brother decided they needed reinforcements.

"We'll have to get some help and then try to herd that little thing down to the barnyard," Dad said.

My father spent the next several days lining up a few of the neighbors—although to me, they didn't exactly seem like neighbors because they all lived at least a mile away—but finally "Operation Last Resort," as Ingman had begun to call it, was set for the next morning.

As it turned out, the effort had been for nothing.

In the evening after we finished milking, I went to the barnyard to change the gates around. I looked toward the Bluff, and for a few seconds, I wondered if I was actually seeing what I thought I was seeing.

As she had done every morning and night for almost two weeks, the cow was once again coming down to the barn.

But this time she wasn't alone.

Walking beside her was a black and white miniature of herself.

I ran across the barnyard to the door.

"Daddy! Come quick!"

My father was in the middle of rinsing the milkers. Dad turned off the vacuum valve, and with my brother right behind him, hurried out to the barnyard.

"What's the matter?" he asked.

"There!" I said, pointing in the direction of the cow and calf.

Dad and Ingman turned toward the lane.

"Hmmmmphhh," my father said, "if that doesn't take the cake."

A few minutes later, the cow walked into the barn.

And so did the calf.

It was as if the little heifer had been going into the barn every day since she was born.

Dad pulled off his chore cap and scratched his head. "I've been farmin' for a lot of years, but it's the first time I've ever seen anything like that."

"I suppose the cow was getting tired of climbing the Bluff," Ingman said.

Dad replaced his chore cap. "I don't know if the cow was getting tired of it, but I sure was."

"How come she had her calf up there, anyway?" I asked. "None of our other cows have done that."

"I have no idea," Dad said. "Maybe she wanted to be the first one to show her baby what life was like from on top of the world."

Maybe so.

But I could tell that as far as Dad and Ingman were concerned, with a little bit of luck, she would also be the last one.

✶✶✶✶✶✶✶✶✶✶✶✶✶✶

~ 17 ~
Dad's Favorite Recipe

The rain had started right after breakfast. Since Dad couldn't cut hay or take a load of corn and oats to the feed mill because the cow feed would get wet in the back of the truck, he decided to go into town after dinner to buy twine string and hydraulic fluid. Often when Dad went to town, I went with him, but today, Mom said I had to stay home and help her clean out the kitchen cupboards. "I'm having Ladies' Aid here next week, and I don't want to leave all of the cleaning for your sister to do," she said.

I wasn't sure why Mom thought the cupboards should be cleaned. The other times the Ladies' Aid had met at our house, none of them had ever opened the kitchen cupboards and looked inside.

But—once Mom got an idea like that into her head—the idea was there to stay. While the rain fell steadily outside the open kitchen window, drenching the trees and the grass and making puddles in the driveway, I used a chair to climb on the counter so I could reach the shelves at the top. As I removed boxes of baking soda and all-spice and cornstarch and cinnamon, and bottles of maraschino cherries and bags of walnuts, Mom took them from me and set them on the table.

When the shelves were empty, I wiped out the cupboard, and then my mother handed everything back to me so I could put it away.

"All right," she said, "now we're going to start on the dish cupboard."

She put the stopper in the drain, turned on the hot water and reached for the bottle of dish soap.

"Why are you doing that?" I asked.

"Because we're going to wash all of the dishes before we put them back."

"We're going to wash *all* of the dishes?"

"Well, no," Mom replied. "Not all of them. Just the ones we don't use very often."

"How come?" I said.

"So they'll be clean the next time I want to use them."

It was bad enough I had to dry the dishes we used every day, but drying dishes we hardly ever used seemed like a waste of time to me.

"But," I said, "you always wash the dishes you don't use very often *right before you use them.*"

"I just want to make sure everything is clean," Mom said.

An hour later, while my mother washed a rectangular clear-glass dish with a rectangular cover that she said was meant to hold a whole pound of butter, I looked out the kitchen window and saw the pickup truck drive past the garage. "Dad's home!" I said.

"So soon?" Mom responded as she rinsed the cover to the butter dish. I could only take my mother's word for it that it was a butter dish because we had never, ever put out a whole pound of butter at one time.

A few minutes later, Dad came into the house.

"Did you get what you needed?" Mom asked. She reached for a dish towel to dry her hands.

My father took off his 'going to town' cap and set it on the table. The top of the blue-and-white cap was speckled with dark blue spots where rain drops had soaked in. The shoulders of Dad's clean blue short-sleeved chambray shirt were also speckled with dark blue spots.

"I got six more bales of twine, five gallons of hydraulic fluid, some nails, in case I need to fix the calf pens or the barnyard fence, and...this," he said, holding up something which looked like a cross between a meat grinder and a pail.

"You bought an ice cream freezer!" Mom said.

While I hung my wet dishtowel on the little rack with movable arms attached to the wall near the sink, Dad held the pail up in front of him and turned it this way and that, as if to admire his purchase.

"A freezer? That's the funniest-looking freezer I've ever seen," I said. "It looks like a blue bucket with a meat grinder on top."

"They call it a freezer because you make ice cream with it," Dad explained.

"How do you make ice cream?" I asked.

Mom and Dad exchanged surprised glances.

"No, I suppose you wouldn't know, would you," my mother said.

Dad set the blue bucket on the floor by the pantry. "Sunday afternoon, we'll make ice cream, and then you can see how it works."

Today was only Thursday, so Sunday was three whole days away.

"Why do we have to wait until Sunday?" I said. "Why can't we make ice cream tonight? Or tomorrow? Or Saturday?"

"Because I've got work to do. Making ice cream will take pretty much all afternoon," Dad replied.

"Making ice cream will take all afternoon?" I said.

"All afternoon," Dad agreed.

I had trouble believing it would take *all* afternoon to make ice cream. Even when my mother baked lefse at Christmas, a batch didn't take *all* afternoon. Sure, rolling out the flat Norwegian potato pastry was time-consuming, but not quite that time consuming. Mom could make an entire batch in about two hours.

"We've got work to do, too," Mom reminded me. "We have to finish the kitchen cupboards tomorrow. And then Saturday, we'll have to go over the whole house with a fine-tooth comb."

Ah, yes. The Ladies' Aid meeting next week.

How could I have forgotten.

Over the next two days, Mom kept me busy helping her clean the house, and then—just when I thought we were never going to finish cleaning out cupboards, moving furniture and washing windows—it was time to milk the cows Saturday evening.

After we had put the milkers together, Dad took the dipper off the nail where it hung in the milkhouse and skimmed a quart of cream out of the bulk tank that he had installed in the milkhouse not long ago.

"Take this to the house and put it in the refrigerator," he said, handing the jar to me.

The glass jar, filled almost to the rim with thick cream, felt cold against my hands.

"Are you *really* going to make ice cream?" I asked.

All my life, I had been watching my father work around the farm. He knew how to fix machinery and build calf pens and hay racks, and how to plant crops and bale hay and milk cows. But make ice cream?

I had never seen Dad make anything to eat. Except eggs for breakfast. And pancakes. And toast. And coffee. But eggs and pancakes and toast and coffee were different, somehow.

"Yes, we're really going to make ice cream," Dad said. "I've been looking for a freezer for a long time. When I saw this one, it was too good to pass up."

"But *why* do you want to make ice cream?" I asked. "We can buy ice cream at the store."

Many times I had heard my mother say she couldn't believe the amount of ice cream we went through, but you only had to watch my father fill a bowl for a snack after milking to understand why. Of course, I ate my fair share too.

"I haven't made ice cream in years. This will taste much better than what we buy in the store," Dad said.

The ice cream we bought in town came in many flavors. Chocolate and chocolate chip. Strawberry. Neapolitan. Maple nut. I had a hard time deciding which was my favorite flavor because they all tasted so good. Ice cream couldn't get any better. Could it?

The next day after we had eaten dinner, I helped Mom and Loretta wash the dishes and put them away. When the dish had been stowed in the cupboard, I went into the living room to talk to Dad, who was sitting on the davenport, reading the latest issue of the weekly newspaper.

"What time are we going to make ice cream?" I asked.

"Right now," Dad said as he folded the newspaper.

My father went into the kitchen, squirted some dish soap into the sink and turned on the hot water. "Seeing as we're making something to eat, I suppose we'd better make sure our ice cream maker is clean," he said.

In the meantime, my mother had sat down by the kitchen table. "Don't you need a recipe, Roy?" she asked. "Didn't they include one with the ice cream freezer?"

Dad paused as he rinsed the tall narrow silver can that went in the middle of the bucket. He shook his head and tapped his temple with one forefinger. "Got the recipe right here," he said. "Best one I've ever used."

"You know the recipe for ice cream by heart?" I said.

"Sure do," Dad replied.

As if Dad's knowing how to make ice cream wasn't enough, now he was saying he didn't even need a recipe? Mom was the only person I knew who didn't need a recipe, but that was just when she was making cake or bread or lefse.

My father finished drying the ice cream maker and then opened the cupboard.

"What are you looking for?" Mom asked.

"Whatever I can find," he replied.

I watched as Dad pushed aside boxes and bottles.

What he ended up finding was the maraschino cherries and walnuts.

"Now we need a pan," Dad said. He rummaged around in the cupboard until he found the pan he wanted.

"What's the pan for?" I asked.

Dad set the pan on the counter. "We have to heat up the milk and sugar and eggs first. And while that's cooling, we'll go out and get our ice."

"Milk? I thought this was going to be ice cream."

"It is," Dad said, "but if you used all cream, when it freezes, it would be almost too hard to eat. Well, you could eat it, but it would be just about impossible to scoop it out of the container."

Dad poured the milk into the pan and added some sugar. Next, he took a carton of eggs out of the refrigerator. He selected several eggs, cracked them open, separated the yolks from the whites, put the yolks in a small bowl, got out the egg beater, and started beating the egg yolks. When he was finished, he used the beater to stir the yolks into the milk.

"How long does that have to cook?" I asked.

"Not long," Dad replied. "Just long enough to heat it up good."

He turned the burner on and started stirring the mixture in the pan, using the metal spoon that was flat across the bottom. We had received the spoon as a Christmas present from our milk hauler one year.

A little while later, when bubbles had formed around the edge and the mixture had begun to simmer, he turned the burner off.

"Now we need our ice," he said.

I followed my father to the machine shed where he took six plastic pails of ice from the freezer. On the day he had brought the ice cream maker home, I had helped him carry out the pails of water.

Dad had built a little room in the shed for the chest freezer, and then, with Ingman's help, had moved the freezer from the porch and into the shed. Mom said she would have liked to keep the freezer in the porch except there wasn't much room for her to get through with her crutches. Dad said it would be easier to build a room in the machine shed than to build onto the porch.

"I need a feed sack, too," Dad said, heading for the granary.

"Why do you need a feed sack?" I asked.

"So I can crush the ice."

Dad sorted through the pile of burlap on the granary floor, found one of the newer feed sacks, took it outside and shook it, and headed back to the machine shed.

As the cloud of dust from the feed sack swirled around me, I sneezed. Feed dust sometimes made me sneeze. I hurried to catch up with Dad. In the machine shed, he opened the feed sack, rolled it back part way, turned one of the pails upside down in the sack and tapped it on the ground. 'Ka-chink!' went the ice as it fell out of the pail.

After all of the pails were empty, Dad went to the workbench and picked up the sledge hammer. He gathered the sides of the burlap bag together, took the hammer and began pounding on the feed sack.

When he was finished, Dad set the bag of crushed ice in the shade near the shed.

By the time we arrived back in the kitchen, the milk-sugar-and-egg mixture had cooled to room temperature. Dad poured the contents of the pan into one of Mom's big mixing bowls and added the cream and some vanilla. He poured it all into the silver part of the ice cream maker and then reached into the cupboard for a bowl, got a knife out of the drawer, and cut the jar of cherries and half the bag of walnuts into little pieces. He dumped the bowl of cherries and walnuts into the silver can.

"What's that thing called?" I asked, as he picked up the device which went in the middle of the ice cream maker. It was rectangular and had square holes up and down the length of it.

"This is the paddle. Or sometimes it's called a dasher. It's what stirs the ice cream as it freezes," Dad explained.

He put the cover on the silver can, set it down inside the ice cream freezer bucket and put the section over the top that had a handle on it.

"We might as well go out to the machine shed and sit in the shade to do this," he said, as he picked up the ice cream freezer and headed for the porch.

In the afternoons, the silver maple by the gas barrel shaded the front of the machine shed.

"Oh," Dad said. "I almost forgot. Grab that box of salt that's up in the cupboard and bring it with you."

"What's the salt for?"

"You have to put salt on the ice to make it melt. That's what helps the ice cream freeze," he explained.

After we got out to the machine shed, Dad asked me to bring the milk stool from the barn. He set the ice cream freezer in the shade and sat down on the milk stool. Then he put a layer of crushed ice in the bottom of the bucket, sprinkled some salt on it, added more ice and more salt, more ice, more salt.

"You're supposed to use rock salt, but this'll do the job," he said.

"What's rock salt?"

"Just what it sounds like—salt that's in big chunks."

"Now what do you have do?" I asked.

"Turn this handle until the ice cream starts to freeze," Dad replied.

"How long will that take?"

"Quite a while."

I sat on the ground and watched as my father turned the handle on the ice cream freezer. He cranked and cranked and cranked, and then cranked some more.

In the branches of the silver maple overhead, sparrows and robins twittered and sang. While he worked, we talked about how robins build their nests, and what it was like when they had made ice cream when Dad was a kid, and where were the best places to find blackberries besides the Bluff, and why cows hide their babies after they're born.

As Dad continued cranking, I went to the milkhouse once to get a drink of water.

At another point, I went out to check Dusty's pail. The pony had drank almost all of her water, so I took the pail to the milkhouse to rinse it and fill it up again.

When I came back from filling the pony's bucket, at long last, Dad stopped turning the handle.

"It's almost finished," he said. "Here, want to give it a try?"

I grasped the handle and pushed and pulled, and pulled and pushed, until I had made it go around a couple of times.

"Hard work, isn't it," Dad said. He picked up the ice cream maker, and I followed him back to the house. He set the bucket on the counter, took the cover off the silver part and removed the paddle.

"Here," he said, reaching into the drawer for a teaspoon, "taste it and tell me what you think."

My father watched as I licked the spoon. "Is it any good?" he asked.

I scraped more of the ice cream off the paddle.

This was like nothing I had ever tasted—creamy and sweet and full of bits of cherries and walnuts. 'Good' didn't begin to describe it. Compared to Dad's ice cream, the ice cream we bought at the store tasted like...it tasted like...well... like plain, old ice cubes.

"This is yummmmmm-eeeeee!" I said, when I had eaten the second spoonful.

Dad grinned. "I was hoping you'd like it."

He pulled another teaspoon from the drawer, scooped up some ice cream and popped the spoon into his mouth.

"Yup," he said, "my favorite recipe still works."

Dad set the spoon in the sink and glanced at the kitchen clock. "Well, look at that. It's almost time to put the cows in and feed them."

Time to feed the cows? It couldn't be almost time to feed the cows.

I turned to look at the clock. And sure enough. It was almost time to feed the cows. We had started making ice cream right after the dinner dishes were done—and now it was nearly five o'clock.

"Is the ice cream all finished?" I asked.

"Not quite," Dad said. "We're going to wrap a towel around it and let it sit in the ice while we put the cows in."

Later on, after we had put the cows in the barn and fed them and had eaten supper, my father dished up the ice cream while my sister set the bowls on the table.

"What do you think of my favorite recipe?" Dad asked.

"Deeeeeee-licious," Mom said. "You just can't buy ice cream that tastes like this."

"It *is* delicious," Loretta said.

"*Very* delicious," Ingman added.

"And it took all afternoon to make!" I said, spooning up another bite of ice cream.

My big sister smiled. "It's like they say, 'good things come to those who wait.'"

That first batch of ice cream was only one of many. Sometimes Dad added crushed chocolate chips. Sometimes he added fresh fruit, such as strawberries or blackberries or peaches. Occasionally he repeated the maraschino cherry-and-walnut combination.

But no matter what Dad added to his favorite recipe, every batch seemed better than the last.

Of course, every batch still also took all afternoon to make.

Loretta was right, though, I think.

Good things *do* come to those who wait.

At least when homemade ice cream is involved.

****

A recipe for making homemade ice cream (without an ice cream maker!) is included in Appendix A.

~ 18 ~
A-Hayin' We Will Go…

I pushed myself up on tiptoes and pulled the plates out of the cupboard. Dad would be coming home any time now, and when he did, we would eat dinner. The plates, which we kept on the second shelf, were white with orange, red and yellow flowers. Mom said the flowers were chrysanthemums, although to me, they looked like daisies.

My mother stood by the stove, stirring together ground beef, tomato sauce, brown sugar and ketchup. At school we called the mixture Sloppy Joes, but at home we called it barbecue. Mom had made potato salad from the boiled potatoes left over from supper last night, and the smell of the chopped onion she put into the salad still hung in the air.

"Dad's here," Mom announced.

I set the plates on the table and turned to look out the kitchen window. It was a beautiful summer day. Warm. Sunny. Breezy. "Perfect haying weather," Dad had said at breakfast this morning. The dew had dried off quickly, and before dinner, he had gone to the hayfield on our other place to get a head start on raking hay.

In my opinion, it was also perfect pony-riding weather, but since Dad had a field of hay cut and had already started to rake, I knew I would be busy for the afternoon, helping him bale hay. That's why he had taught me how to drive the tractor in the first place, so that when Ingman was working the day shift at the creamery, Dad wouldn't have to bale by himself. Driving the 460 Farmall was a whole lot of fun—almost as much fun as riding my pony.

Ever since I was old enough to know what a pony was, I had wanted one, but after I finally talked Mom into giving her permission, she still hadn't liked the idea. For one thing, she said, horses were dangerous. And for another thing, we already had enough animals to feed, never mind a pony who wouldn't pay her own way. And not only that, Mom also said she was afraid I would waste my time fooling around with the pony instead of doing my chores.

I had asked what Mom meant by saying a pony wouldn't pay its own way, and she had replied that a pony would not be useful—that it would just be a pet.

Personally, I didn't see anything wrong with being a pet. All of the cows were Dad's pets, at least that's what the cows thought, and so did Dad, judging by the way he talked to them and brushed them and scratched their foreheads as he was feeding hay.

But when I had pointed out that the cows were Dad's pets, it still hadn't changed my mother's opinion about a pony.

As for neglecting my chores, after Mom gave her permission, one of the rules was that I must never ask to ride the pony when there was other work to do. "If I find out you're wasting time with that pony, we're going to give her away," Mom had said.

So you can see why I didn't dare mention that I wanted to ride Dusty this afternoon.

As I got out the knives, forks and spoons, I heard the screen door open.

"How soon until dinner is ready?" Dad asked. He stood in the porch and peered into the kitchen.

"Right now," Mom said. "All I have to do is dish up the barbecue and take the potato salad out of the refrigerator."

"Guess I'd better get washed up then," Dad replied. He took off his cap and headed for the bathroom.

In a few minutes, my father returned to the kitchen, smelling of the Ivory soap he had used to wash his hands and face.

Mom set the potato salad in the middle of the table. "What time will the hay be ready?" she asked.

Dad pulled out his pocket watch.

"Well, let's see," he said, "I suppose I'll be ready to bale about 2:30. I've still got some hay left to rake."

My mother turned to me. "You'll have to go over to the field with Dad when we're done eating dinner," she said.

I liked helping my father bale hay. And I knew haying was important because if we didn't bale hay, the cows wouldn't have anything to eat during the winter, and neither would Dusty. The part I didn't like about helping Dad was the waiting. If I went with Dad right after dinner, then I would have to wait for at least an hour—or maybe even two hours—with nothing to do except sit in the shade while my father drove up and down the windrows with the hay rake.

Oh, sure, I would have Needles to keep me company. Or at least I would have the dog to keep me company part of the time, after he grew tired of following the tractor and wanted to rest.

And I could go for a walk down the dirt road that ran past our other place. The purple flowers which smelled like lemons were starting to bloom, and there were clumps of white flowers that reminded me of the lace on one of my big sister's blouses and bunches of yellow flowers Dad said were called brown-eyed Susans. I couldn't pick any of the wildflowers, though, because they would be wilted by the time we were ready to go home.

Or I could bring a book with me. My favorite books were about horses. But if I brought a book, where would I put it while I was driving the tractor? And if I left my book under a shade tree at the end of the field, what if I forgot it when we were ready to go home?

"Nope," Dad said, interrupting my thoughts, "she doesn't have to come with me when I go back to rake hay."

My mother looked across the table at Dad. "She most certainly does have to go with you. How are you going to bale without her? Well, I know you *can* bale without her, but you won't get as much done. And I'd rather not have hay left in windrows in the field overnight."

Dad speared a couple of dill pickles with his fork and handed the dish to me. "She doesn't have to, I'm telling you."

My mother drew herself up straight. "And I'm telling you that she does," she said.

I looked back and forth between Mom and Dad.

This was getting interesting.

"She does *not* have to come with me," Dad said. He glanced in my direction, and his right eye closed in the briefest of winks.

"I saw that," Mom said. "Why are you winking."

"She does not have to come with *me*," Dad repeated.

My mother shook her head in defeat. "Okay, I give up. Why not?"

Dad pursed his lips in the way that meant he was trying not to smile. "She doesn't have to come with me because..." He paused to make sure Mom and I were both listening. "Because—she can ride Dusty over."

It took a moment for my father's words to sink in.

Then I realized what he had actually said.

Ride Dusty! To the field so we could bale hay!

I threw a happy smile in Dad's direction. He winked again, and this time it was an all-out wink and not one he was trying to hide from Mom.

"Ride Dusty?" my mother said. "I don't know if that's such a good idea—"

"I can't see why I didn't think of it before," Dad continued. "If she starts out at two o'clock, by the time they get over there, the hay will be ready."

"And what, may I ask, is she going to do with Dusty while you're baling?" Mom inquired.

"Tie her to a tree," Dad replied.

Tie her to a tree! Of *course* I could tie Dusty to a tree! Large trees grew along the edge of the fields on the other place. There were oak trees and maple trees and wild cherry trees...

"Hmmmm...," Mom said, "I really don't know..."

Dad reached for the potato salad. "It'll work out just perfect. Besides, then she'll be able to help you with the dishes instead of sitting in the field watching me rake hay."

"Please Mom?" I said.

My mother drew a deep breath and then let it out slowly. "I guess it is kind of a waste of time for you to sit in the hayfield with nothing to do. So maybe it would be all right. As long as you are very careful and promise to get off and hold onto Dusty's halter if a car comes along."

"I promise!"

I wasn't worried about keeping my promise. Cars hardly ever traveled the road going to our other place. During the winter, a car might use the road once a month, although in the summer, it was probably more like once a week.

After we had finished eating and Dad and Needles had left for the other place again, I helped Mom clear the table and wash the dishes. Even though Dusty and I wouldn't have to leave for another thirty minutes, right after I put the last dish away, I went outside to bring a fresh pail of water for the pony. Dad had said I should check to see if Dusty wanted a drink before we left, otherwise she would be mighty thirsty by the time we got home again.

Dusty got a drink, and then I led her to the machine shed, tied the end of the lead rope to the door track, and took my brush and my curry comb and brushed the dirt off her. I had named the pony Dusty because her brown coloring with lighter dapples made her look like someone had dusted her with a powder puff. But the name fit in other ways, too, because she also liked to roll in the dirt.

A little while later, with a lead rope looped over my pony's shoulders, we started out. Not long after I had gotten the pony, my father tried putting a bridle on her, but she had fought the bit and never could get used to it, so I had taken to riding her with only a rope clipped to her halter.

At the bottom of the driveway, Dusty and I turned left onto the road leading to our other place. The pony's hooves made a steady clippety-clop, clippety-clop as I rode through the shade of the tall oak and wild black cherry and silver maple trees growing along the bank. Dusty's pasture lay just beyond the trees, and when I went to get my pony on hot summer days, I often found her grazing the hillside in the shade of the silver maples that grew along the edge of the lawn.

Although I was riding bareback, and only had a rope for reins, I felt like a cowboy out on an adventure. Dusty and I were not riding the range to herd cows, but we were on our way to do the next best thing: help Dad bale hay for the cows.

A short way down the road, the trees ended. Dusty swished her tail and shook her head to chase away the flies that had followed us out into the hot sunshine. Each time Dusty's head bobbed, her thick, white mane flopped up and down. Dad said it was a half a mile from the bottom of our driveway until the road made a sharp turn, and that it was another quarter of a mile from where the road turned until the first field driveway at our other place.

In hardly any time at all, we arrived at the corner.

I leaned forward to hug the pony's neck. "Good girl, Dusty, we're almost there," I said.

I sat up straight, and my hands were wet and sticky with horse sweat. Sweat trickled down the side of my face too.

"Hot out here, isn't it," I said.

The pony snorted, as if to answer me, although it was more likely a fly had landed on her nose.

A few minutes later, we entered the shade of the oak trees growing on the hill across the road from the hayfield. Thick brush covered the wooded hillside next to us, and as we went past, I looked for the wintergreen Dad had showed me one Christmas when we had gone to our other place to cut a tree, although I didn't catch even a glimpse of it. There were too many other green leaves for me to see the small wintergreen plants growing close to the ground.

At the top of the hill, we came around the curve, and then I could see the field driveway. I could also hear the engine of the Super C Farmall, which meant that Dad was still raking hay.

By the time I rode into the field, my father was almost finished with the next to the last windrow. When he reached the end of the field, he stopped the tractor and got off.

"Where should I tie Dusty?" I asked.

"I've been thinking about that," Dad said as he walked toward us. He pointed to a maple tree in the corner of the field only a few steps away. "That maple is probably the best. The others have such big trunks."

The maple tree was really a cluster of smaller trees growing in one clump. I slid off the pony's back, and as I led her to the maple tree, I saw Needles sitting in the shade of a couple of jack pine situated between the field and the road. His ears were perked, and as he panted, his mouth opened in a delighted grin.

Dad got back on the tractor, and while he made the turn to continue raking the last windrow, I unclipped one end of the lead rope from the halter so I could tie Dusty to the tree. Even before I finished knotting the rope, the pony began to pick the tall grass that tickled her chin.

In a little while, Dad finished the windrow and parked the tractor and the rake at the end of the field near the driveway. He got off the tractor, removed his cap and stood facing into the breeze to cool his face. "I see it didn't take Dusty long to make herself to home," he said.

My plump brown pony stood beneath the maple tree, head down, white tail swishing from side to side, jaws working furiously as she pulled the long grass and chewed it.

"Will she be okay here by herself?" I asked.

"She's so busy, she probably won't even know we're gone," Dad said.

When my father started the 460 Farmall to line up the tractor and baler on the windrow, the pony lifted her head to watch, although she soon went back to eating.

While I drove the four-sixty along windrows of hay as tall as Dad's knees, the pony stood beneath the maple tree, either picking grass or relaxing in the shade with one hind foot cocked. By the time we had finished the second load, Dusty had eaten all of the grass she could reach.

We parked the tractor and baler, disconnected the wagon, and then Dad and I went over to see Dusty.

The pony was standing with her eyes closed, dozing.

"What do you think, Dusty?" my father asked.

At the sound of his voice, the pony woke up and nickered.

My father smiled and patted the pony's rump. "That's what I think, too. It's time to go home."

Dad turned back toward the tractor. "I'm gonna cover the baler and put a can over the muffler—in case it rains you know, which I don't think it will—but anyway, if you start out now, by the time I come with the first load, you'll be on the flat and away from the hill."

"What's wrong with being on the hill?" I asked.

"It's kind of narrow and the load takes up a lot of room," Dad said. "I wouldn't want Dusty to be scared and have no place to go. You can't get down in the ditch."

There was no ditch to speak of on the hill, only a bank and trees growing right next to the road. I was pretty sure the pony wouldn't be afraid of the tractor and a load of hay. After all, she saw tractors and loads of hay almost every day during the summer. But, if Dad wanted us to go, we would go.

I untied the lead rope, looped it over Dusty's shoulders, grabbed hold of her mane, threw one leg over her back and pulled myself up.

Soon we were headed in the direction we came, clippety-clop, clippety-clop, up the hill and into the shade.

We were halfway home when Dad and Needles passed us with the load. The wagon squeaked and groaned under the weight of the hay. Needles trotted next to the front tire of the tractor, his pink tongue dangling from the side of his mouth, looking as happy as a dog could be. My father took off his cap and waved as he drove by.

A few minutes later, our adventure was almost over as Dusty and I climbed the hill of our driveway.

After we arrived in the yard, I rode to the gate leading into the pony's pasture, took off her halter and turned her loose. She went to her pail to get a drink, raising her head after a few sips to let the water dribble out of her mouth before taking another drink.

The pony finished drinking and walked to a spot of bare dirt. In slow motion, her legs buckled beneath her, and she collapsed with a heavy sigh. Moments later, she rolled onto her back, feet waving in the air as she wriggled in the dirt.

Dad came up beside me. "Hah!" he said. "If that isn't just like a horse. Work hard all afternoon, and then roll to dry off the sweat."

Dusty scrambled to her feet and shook herself, causing a cloud of dust to fly up around her.

My father laughed. "It was an honest day's work, wasn't it, Dusty."

He turned to me. "She was good help this afternoon, don't you think?"

I looked at Dusty, who was once again picking grass and swishing her white tail.

"Oh, yes, Daddy," I said, "she was *really* good help."

At supper that evening, my father made a point of telling my mother how well it had worked for me to ride Dusty to the hayfield.

"They got there just when I was finishing up the last windrow," he said. "And Dusty was such a good pony. She acted like she'd spent her whole life waiting while we baled hay."

"And there weren't any cars along the way, either," I said.

"And Dusty wasn't one bit afraid of the tractor and the load when I drove past," Dad added.

My mother used one hand to fluff her dark, curly hair as she looked back and forth between Dad and I. "I'm glad to hear everything went all right," she said. "I'll have you know that I sat here and worried about it all afternoon."

"What were you worried about?" Dad inquired.

"It's a long way for her to ride Dusty," she said, "and if anything happened, nobody would be there to help her."

"That little pony is the best pony in the whole world," my father said. "You don't have to worry."

In the following weeks, whenever Dad needed a tractor driver, I would ride Dusty to the hayfield. And each time, I could hardly believe I was riding my pony *and* doing my chores.

After a while, Mom even came right out and admitted Dusty was making herself extremely useful and was now more than just a pet who didn't pay her own way.

And that—it seemed to me—was the very best part of all.

****

~ 19 ~
For Medicinal Purposes

D ad finished tying his shoelaces and stood up. "Time to milk the cows, kiddo, so let's get out to the barn," he said. As I slipped into my chore boots, I could still smell the coffee he had brewed in the percolator sitting on the stove burner. Dad always made coffee first thing in the morning. I followed my father through the porch, out the door and down the steps.

"Look at that," he said, pointing to the lawn between the house and the machine shed. "We've got diamonds today."

The sun was shining through the trees and striking the dew on the grass in such a way that each blade sparkled. I turned my head so I could see more of the lawn. And then I noticed something else.

"Hey!" I said, "I think we have a new baby!"

"What?" Dad asked. He looked in the direction I was pointing.

"Jeepers," he said, "I believe you're right."

Dad and I headed across the yard. The cow was just on the other side of the fence beneath the overhanging branches of the silver maples lining the edge of the lawn. She was one of our Holstein heifers, and as we got closer to the fence, we could see that she had given birth to her first calf on the sidehill behind the house. For as far back as I could remember, none of our cows ever had a calf so close to the house.

The sidehill was Dusty's pasture, but Dad had said we should put the pony into the little pasture behind the pole barn for a few days and let the cows go in Dusty's pasture at night to pick it down, seeing as there was more grass than my pony could eat by herself.

"Is it a girl or a boy?" I asked after we had climbed through the barbed wire fence.

The calf was still wet and not strong enough yet to stand up. The cow wasn't standing up yet, either. When we moved toward them, the baby shook its head and snorted, as if to say, "What happened? Where am I?"

Dad reached down to lift the tail.

"It's a girl," he said.

My father picked the calf up and set her in front of her mother. The cow went to work, dragging her tongue along the calf's back, while the baby braced herself to keep from being pushed over onto her side.

"You're a good momma, aren't you," Dad said with a smile.

He turned to me. "We'll just let them be for now. By the time we're done milking, the cow will be up and the baby will be dried off, and then we can bring them into the barn."

An hour and a half later we went back to the pasture after we had finished feeding the cows and doing the milking. The calf was now standing on wobbly legs, but the cow was still lying down in the same place she'd been before we went to the barn.

"You must be tired after all your hard work," Dad commented. As he scratched the top of the cow's forehead, she stretched her neck to lick the leg of his work overalls.

The mother was a mixture of white and black patches. The baby was solid black, except for a white tip on her tail and a small white spot between her eyes.

She was cutest calf I had ever seen.

Of course, every calf that was born on the place was the cutest calf I had ever seen—until the next one was born.

"Daddy?"

"What?"

"How come we never picked a name for this cow?"

It was a rare occurrence when one of our cows went without a name, especially one as nice as this cow. Some of the other Holsteins were jittery and didn't like to be petted, but this one had always enjoyed the attention. For a while, we had called her Betsy, but she just didn't seem like a Betsy. Or an Annabelle. Or a Daisy. Or any of the other names we had tried.

"I don't know why we've never picked a name," Dad said. "Seems like we've never been able to come up with a good one, have we."

"I know what we're going to call her baby," I said.

"What's that?" Dad asked.

"Star."

My father turned his attention to the youngster, who, unsure of this new thing called walking, was standing with her front legs slightly apart.

"Star would be a good name," he said, "seeing as she's got that little white mark on her forehead."

A fly landed on the calf's nose. She shook her head to chase it away and almost lost her balance.

"You sure are a cute little thing," Dad said. "And you know what else? Your grandma's a good milker, and I think your momma's going to be a good milker. And someday, you'll probably be a good milker, too."

"Maaaaah," said the calf. She twitched her ears and flapped her tail up and down. My father patted the top of her head, and her dark-blue eyes with their long black lashes opened wide as she ducked away from his hand.

Dad pulled off his chore cap, put it back on, pulled it off and put it back on. Whenever Dad fiddled with his cap, that meant he was thinking about something.

"Our little baby really ought to drink some of her mother's milk," he said. "She needs the colostrum."

Colostrum, I knew, was the yellow-colored milk cows gave for the first few days after their calves were born. Dad said colostrum helped the babies to grow stronger and kept them from becoming sick.

My father walked around to the other side of the cow. "Let's see if we can get her up," he said.

After a minute or two of urging, with Dad pushing at her rump and me pushing on her shoulder, the cow pulled herself to her knees. But even though she tried, she couldn't quite get her back legs under her enough to stand up.

"Would you go to the barn and get a calf pail?" Dad asked. "Not a regular pail. We need one of the other ones."

We had two kinds of calf pails. One was an ordinary galvanized bucket. The other kind had a metal plug near the bottom that could be taken out and replaced with a large rubber nipple.

"Okay, Daddy," I said.

I scrambled through the fence and trotted across the yard, past the gas barrel, and into the barn. I grabbed one of the pails with a plug in it and then rooted around on the shelf under the milker compressor until I found a rubber nipple.

With the pail in hand, I trotted back across the yard.

"Thank you," Dad said. He took out the plug and attached the nipple. Then he knelt beside the cow, and with the calf bucket tipped at an angle, began to milk her until a couple of inches of colostrum filled the bottom of the pail.

"That's enough for now, otherwise I'll spill it," he said, as he stood up.

Dad put his fingers in the calf's mouth. She began to suck on them, and he slipped the rubber nipple into her mouth next to his fingers. The calf quickly got the idea and was soon busily sucking from the pail.

"Maaaa-aaaah!" she said, sounding both disappointed and surprised when the pail went dry.

Dad repeated the process several times until the calf's hunger was satisfied.

"That should hold her for a little while," he said. "Now let's go to the house and get breakfast. By the time we're finished eating, the cow will probably be on her feet."

When we returned to the pasture forty-five minutes later, the cow was lying down yet.

And so it went all morning long. Dad said I should keep an eye on the cow and that after she got up, we would move them into the barn. But every time I checked on her, she remained the same.

On my last trip before dinner, Dad came out to the pasture too, and then we walked back to the house together.

My mother was in the kitchen, hunting through the utensil drawer. "Is she up yet?" she asked.

Dad shook his head. "Same as she was this morning."

He hung his chore cap on the newel post and headed for the bathroom to wash his hands.

On top of the clothesline pole not far from the kitchen window, a blue jay squawked—thief—thief—thief—thief.

"That blue jay has been around here for a half an hour, and he's really starting to get on my nerves," Mom said, as she pulled the tongs out of the drawer. "And my nerves don't need any more help today, not when we've got a cow that can't get up."

She made her way over to the stove, dipped the tongs into the boiling pot on the front burner and put an ear of sweet corn on a plate.

Every year, Dad planted a garden. Mom said it was 'too big' but Dad said it was 'just right.' The sweet corn was starting to ripen, and this was only our second meal of it for the year. Dad raised the same kind of sweet corn that the canning factories used. The ears were as long as an ear of field corn, and the yellow kernels were almost as sweet and juicy as watermelon. An hour before dinner, Mom had sent me to the garden to pick a dozen ears. I had always thought it was too bad sweet corn didn't grow all year because then we could eat it every day.

In a few minutes, my father returned to the kitchen and sat down by the table.

"I think we should call the vet," Dad said. "Something's not right."

My mother lifted the last ear of sweet corn out of the pot and set it on the plate with the others. "They're usually up right away after they've had their calves. This one's been down a long time," she said as she set the plate of steaming sweet corn in middle of the table.

"Too long. I've been around a lot of cows, but I've never seen one like that," Dad said.

"If I call the vet, what if she's up by the time he gets here?" Mom inquired.

My father shrugged and moved his knife, fork and spoon a little farther from his plate. "What if she's not?"

Mom sat down at her end of the table and folded her hands. I quickly said the table prayer, and then Mom and Dad continued their conversation as if no interruption had taken place.

"I guess we won't know if she's going to be up by the time the vet gets here until he's here," my mother said as she reached for an ear of corn.

"But if she can't ever get up and there's nothing else we can do for her ..." Dad added.

"We'll have to send her for slaughter," Mom said.

All at once, my mouthful of sweet corn lost its flavor. Instead of sweet and juicy, it tasted like soggy cardboard. I hadn't thought about what might happen to the heifer if she couldn't get on her feet.

After dinner, Mom called the vet. I had never seen Dad dial the telephone himself. If my father wanted to talk to someone he asked Mom to dial the number, although most of the time he would rather have my mother make the call for him. Mom said talking on the telephone wasn't Dad's cup of tea. The black plastic telephone stood on a small table in the living room close to my mother's chair.

All afternoon, I watched for the veterinarian's truck. It was almost time to put the cows in for the evening milking when he arrived. He parked his truck by the barn, and as Dad and the vet walked across the yard to the pasture, I followed along.

The vet was taller than Dad, and he was also younger than Dad, maybe about the same age as my big brother. We didn't need the vet very often, but this one had been to our place a couple of times. Dad said he was a good cow vet.

"What do you think is wrong with her?" Dad asked as the three of us stood looking down at the young black and white cow. She tried to get up a couple of times but still only made it as far as her knees before collapsing.

"Can't say for sure," the vet replied, crouching down beside her. "She could have permanent nerve damage. Or it might be that the ligaments haven't tightened up yet or that she has a torn ligament."

"At least she's not down flat," Dad observed. "But what can we do for her?"

The vet glanced up at my father. "I'm sorry to say there's not much we *can* do. Not in the way of medication, anyway. I can give her something in case she's feeling a little weak from being dehydrated. But other than that, I think you'll just have to give her some time."

"How much time?" Dad asked.

It hadn't taken the calf long to figure out that Dad was the source of good things to eat. When she put her forehead against his leg and nudged him, my father absentmindedly patted the top of her head.

The vet stood up. "If the cow's not on her feet in a couple of days, then I would say it's hopeless."

"All right, that's what we'll do then," Dad said. "We'll just give her some time."

"This is going to mean quite a bit of extra work for you because you'll have to haul food and water out here," the vet said. "It's important for her to eat because that will help her get her strength back. And you'll have to milk her by hand too. Are you sure this is what you want to do?"

"I'm sure," Dad replied. "We have to at least give her a chance."

"Okay, then," the vet said. "That's what I thought you'd say. If she hasn't shown any improvement in a couple of days, give me another call."

We watched as he pumped some liquid into the cow's throat; afterwards, we walked with him to his truck. He got in and started the engine, and as he pulled away, he waved. I waved back, and then Dad and I went into the barn.

My father opened the cover of the feed box and put two scoops of cow feed into a calf pail. "Let's see if she'll eat something," he said. "Maybe she's hungry now."

Earlier in the afternoon we had brought feed and water to the heifer. She had drank some of the water, but she hadn't wanted anything to eat.

My father held out the pail of feed. "If you'll take this, I'll fill another pail with water," he said.

Dad and I walked side by side across the yard, each carrying our own pail.

"You know," my father said, "it would be a big help if you could feed and water her three or four times a day. Do you think you could do that?"

I glanced at the pail Dad carried. Dusty sometimes drank two pails of water on a hot day, but a cow, I knew, drank a lot more water than my pony.

"You don't have to carry a big pail of water like this all the way from the barn every time," he said. "You can use one of the calf pails to fill a big pail."

And that's how it became my job to feed and water the heifer. Dad said he would take care of milking her and feeding the calf.

In short order, I figured out that Dad's job was easier than mine. The heifer had little choice in the matter when Dad milked her because she was unable to get up and walk off. And the calf was quite willing to suck from the nipple pail. But I couldn't get the heifer to eat a thing. When I set the bucket of feed in front of her, she sniffed it and turned her head away.

"Maybe she wants some hay instead," Dad suggested.

I went back to the barn and got two flakes of hay, but the heifer turned her head away from that too.

"What am I doing wrong? Why won't she eat?" I said.

The vet had told us it was important for her to eat because eating would help her get better. But even if the heifer didn't starve to death in Dusty's pasture, if she couldn't get to her feet, she would end up in somebody's freezer, cut into little pieces. And I didn't want to think about her being cut up into little pieces.

"You're not doing anything wrong," Dad replied. "She'll probably get hungry during the night and then she'll eat. When you come out here in the morning, I bet the hay will be gone."

"Do you really think so?"

"Yes," Dad said, "I really think so."

I looked at the heifer. She had her legs tucked under her, the way cows do when they're resting comfortably in the shade on a hot day.

Maybe Dad was right. Maybe when I came out in the morning, the hay would be gone.

The next morning I went out to the pasture to feed the heifer, and the pile of hay was in the same place, untouched. But the heifer was gone. And so was her baby.

I was trying to decide how I was going to tell Dad that I had lost the cow when I looked toward the road and saw she had managed to crawl down the hill until she was resting in the shade of another large silver maple. The calf was standing beside her.

I carried the pail of water down the hill and set it in front of her. The heifer drank a little, but when I offered her the feed, she wouldn't even put her nose in the bucket. I went to the top of the hill, picked up the hay and held a flake to my nose, to see if it smelled all right. The hay was damp from laying on the ground overnight, but it just smelled like hay to me, a mixture of alfalfa and clover blossoms.

"Do you want some of this?" I said, setting the hay in front of the heifer where she could reach it. She put her nose down to smell it and then flipped it off to the side.

By afternoon, when Dad and I went out to see how the cow was doing, she still hadn't touched her food.

"If she doesn't eat something pretty soon," Dad muttered, "she'll never get better."

And that's when our campaign began to find something the cow would eat.

We searched the mow for bales of pure alfalfa hay. Dad said second crop would be better than first crop. We eventually found what we were looking for, and yet, when I put a few flakes in front of the heifer, she only ate a couple of wisps.

"Well," Dad said, "that didn't work, did it."

He pulled off his chore cap and then put it back on his head again.

"Go in the house and ask Ma if we can have a bottle of molasses," he said.

"What do we need molasses for?" I wondered.

"We're going to mix it with some feed," he explained.

During the winter, Dad bought molasses by the gallon at the feed mill to drizzle over the hay as a treat for the cows. But the molasses from last winter was long gone.

When I told Mom why I needed a bottle of molasses, she readily agreed. "I hope it works," she said.

After I returned with the molasses, Dad poured half the bottle over a pail of feed. The odor reminded me of the molasses cookies my sister baked.

"Smells good enough to eat, doesn't it," Dad said.

We set the bucket in front of the heifer, but she only licked at it and then gave up.

"What about some grass?" I said.

Dad thought about it for a few moments. "Not grass. Alfalfa."

We stopped by the shed so Dad could get the scythe. Our next stop was the granary for a burlap bag. We climbed into the truck and drove out to the hayfield, and while Dad cut alfalfa with the scythe, I put it into the burlap bag.

A little while later when we set some of the fresh alfalfa in front of the heifer, for a minute there, it looked as though she were going to eat it. But after a few polite mouthfuls, she gave up and rested her chin on the pile.

"Let's go to the mow and get that other bale of hay we found," Dad said. "Maybe she'll like that one better."

I followed my father toward the barn, and as we neared the door, he stopped so abruptly that I almost ran into him.

"That's IT!" he exclaimed, slapping his thigh.

"What's what?" I asked.

"I don't know why I didn't think of it before." He headed for the garden, pulled out his pocket knife and set to work.

"What *are* you doing?" I asked.

"Cutting sweet corn. She's bound to like this."

Since the cow hadn't wanted to eat anything else, I wasn't at all sure she would eat sweet corn. I kept it to myself, though. I didn't want to hurt Dad's feelings.

A little while later, I set an armful of green sweet corn in front of the heifer. She pulled a stalk into her mouth and began chewing, quickly finished the first stalk, and then curled her tongue around another one and pulled it toward her mouth.

"Look at that!" Dad said.

"She likes it!" I said.

After we had given her the alfalfa, she had eaten a few polite mouthfuls. There was nothing polite about the way she was eating the sweet corn.

My father showed me how to cut the stalks and put one of his old pocket knives in the barn by the milker compressor where I could find it when I needed it.

Within two days, the heifer had consumed a half a garden's worth of sweet corn.

"I guess that mystery is solved, isn't it," Dad said when I put yet another helping in front of the heifer.

"What mystery?"

"Now we know what her name is."

Dad and I looked at each other.

"Sweetcorn!" we both said in the same breath.

Soon the heifer also began eating the hay and ground feed that I brought out for her. And then one morning when I gave her breakfast, to my utter astonishment, she got to her feet.

I set the pail of feed down and ran for the barn, my shoes hardly touching the ground.

"Daddy! Daddy!"

"What's wrong?" Dad asked, as he came out of the milkhouse, holding a milker bucket in one hand.

"Sweetcorn is standing up," I said.

When we arrived in the pasture, Sweetcorn had her nose in the pail, eating feed, and the calf, Star, was nursing contentedly, her tail flapping up and down and wiggling from side to side.

"Well," Dad said, "isn't that just about the prettiest sight you've ever seen."

Although Sweetcorn was weak at first, and thinner than she should have been, by the end of the day, she was walking around Dusty's pasture almost as if nothing had ever been wrong with her.

After that, her recovery was like someone had waved a magic wand over her.

The vet stopped by a few days later. "I was in the area, so I wanted to see how your cow is doing," he explained.

Dad was at the back of the farm fixing a fence, but the cows were in the barnyard.

"There she is," I said, pointing to the young cow.

The vet climbed over the barnyard fence. The other cows scattered when he approached, but Sweetcorn stood there calmly as the vet ran his hand over her sleek black-and-white flank.

"To look at her, you'd never know she'd been down. What did you do to help her?" he asked.

"We fed her sweet corn," I said.

The vet looked at me, eyebrows raised. "Sweet corn? Ears of sweet corn?"

"No—we cut the stalks, ears and all," I said. "She ate almost the whole garden, too, before she got better. We didn't get hardly any of it. Mom used to say Dad's garden was too big. But this year she says it wasn't quite big enough."

The vet grinned. "I'm going to have to remember that the next time someone has a cow down. I didn't know you could use sweet corn for medicinal purposes."

Actually—I didn't, either.

Before this, I had only thought of sweet corn as delicious people food. Especially when it was covered with melted butter and sprinkled with salt.

But I never, ever dreamed sweet corn could turn out to be just what the doctor ordered.

****

~ 20 ~
Better Butter

S ummer vacation had ended more than a month ago, and a few of the trees I could see from the classroom window were beginning to turn gold and red and copper. At the front of the room, our teacher stood beside the map of Wisconsin with a long wooden pointer in her hand.

Wisconsin was one of several maps along the top of the blackboard that could be pulled down or rolled up like a window shade. On the first day of school, the teacher had informed us we would be studying the United States this year, and that we would start with our very own state.

The teacher tapped the pointer on the blackboard to make sure we were all listening.

"Let's review. What is our state known for?" she asked. "Or maybe a better question is—what is our state's nickname?"

The only sound was the creaking of a few chairs as some of my classmates shifted in their seats.

"Does anyone remember our state's nickname?" the teacher asked, reaching up to straighten the large white collar of her navy blue dress. Each day, our teacher wore a dress and a pair of low-heeled pumps to match. Today she was wearing navy blue shoes trimmed with white scallops.

After a pause, several hands went up.

"Wisconsin is the Badger State," said one of my classmates.

The teacher nodded. "Yes. And what else? Something we have in the cafeteria every morning."

"Milk?" said another of my classmates.

"Let's put on our thinking caps," the teacher said. "We're trying to think of the nickname for our state that has something to do with milk…"

"America's Dairyland!" said a couple of students at the same time.

"That's right," the teacher said. "And why is Wisconsin known as America's Dairyland?"

I raised my hand. "Because we have so many dairy farms."

"Yes, that's correct. Wisconsin is known as America's Dairyland because we have lots of dairy farms. How many of you live on a dairy farm?" she wondered.

My hand shot up, and so did the hands of at least half the other kids in my class.

"How many of you farmers have made butter?" the teacher asked.

All the hands went down, including mine. I had heard my mother talk about churning butter when she was a girl, but that was as close as I had gotten to doing it myself. Mom said butter was made with a butter churn, which she described as looking like a narrow wooden barrel with a broom handle sticking out of the top. To churn the butter, you moved the handle up and down, she said.

"Has anybody else made butter?" our teacher continued, looking around the room, "even if you don't live on a dairy farm?"

No other hands went up.

"How many of you would like to *try* making butter?" the teacher asked.

I looked at the girl who sat across from me, and we both grinned.

"I would," I said.

"Me, too," said the girl who sat across from me.

"I would! I would! Me, too! Me, too!" came a chorus of voices.

The teacher smiled. "I thought so. What is butter made from?"

Of course I knew the answer. My mother had talked about churning butter, and my brother worked at the creamery. My hand went up and so did a few others. The teacher called on another girl.

"Butter is made from cream," the girl said.

"And what do you have to do with cream to make butter?" the teacher asked.

This time, I found myself all alone with my hand raised.

"You have to mix it up for a really, *really* long time," I explained.

"That's right," the teacher said. She looked around the class. "Who could bring some cream for us? We need four people to bring a half a quart, along with a quart jar and a cover for the jar."

I was pretty sure Mom and Dad wouldn't mind if I brought a half a quart of cream to school. I knew what a half a quart looked like. My mother canned pickles and tomatoes and jelly and jam during the summer. The pickles and tomatoes were put into quart jars. Mom put jelly and jam into pint jars because she said the half-pint jars made for jelly and jam would only last through a couple of breakfasts. One pint, I knew, was a half a quart.

I raised my hand. "I can bring some cream."

The teacher looked around the room once again. "And who else?" she asked.

For a while, no one said anything. Then, as the seconds ticked by and I had started to think I was going to be the only one, three other kids volunteered.

"Good. This way, we'll have two whole quarts of cream and four quart jars. We're going to make our butter tomorrow, and since we don't have a butter churn, we will shake the quart jars, instead. So be sure you put the cream into a quart jar, and be sure to put a cover on the jar, don't just put aluminum foil or wax paper over it," the teacher said. "Can you all remember what you're supposed to bring?"

"A pint of cream in a quart jar and be sure to put a cover on the jar," said one of the other kids who had volunteered to bring cream.

"Yes," the teacher said, "and please remember the rest of us are counting on you. If you don't bring the cream, we won't be able to make butter."

The final bell rang in a little while, and during the long bus ride home, I kept reminding myself to tell Mom about the cream as soon as I got in the house. My mother never forgot anything, so I knew she wouldn't let me leave for school the next morning without cream.

After getting off the bus, I nearly ran up the hill of our driveway. A cool breeze blew out of the west, but the sunshine felt warm on my face and arms. Last night at supper, Dad said he wouldn't be surprised if we woke up one morning soon to find frost.

When I reached the top of the driveway Needles came to greet me, his tail going in circles. I gave him a hasty pat on the head and then hurried up the porch steps.

"Mom!" I shouted as I went into the kitchen. "I need some cream!"

My mother was sitting by the table, peeling potatoes for supper.

"What?" she asked. "Cream? Why you do need cream?"

I put my books on the table. "We're going to make butter! In school! Tomorrow! I promised to bring cream! It's okay if I bring cream isn't it? Please, please, please? Can't I please bring some cream? I mean, may I bring some cream? I promised I would…"

My mother hesitated as she considered my request. "Lucky for you the milk hauler didn't come this morning."

I had forgotten all about the milk hauler. If he had picked up our milk today, then we wouldn't have any cream for a while. The milk hauler came every other day to empty the bulk tank.

"Not that it really matters if the milk hauler came," my mother continued. "You'd just have to wait until tomorrow morning."

"Is it okay then?" I asked.

"Of course it's all right. If it's for school, then you shall have cream."

I pulled out one of the chairs by the table and sat down. "I need to put it in a quart jar too. And I need a cover for the jar."

"A quart jar?" Mom replied.

"So we can shake it," I explained. "That's how our teacher said we're going to make butter. Everybody who's bringing cream is supposed to bring it in a quart jar and put a cover on the jar."

My mother selected another potato. Usually it was my job to go into the basement to get potatoes for supper, so Mom must have asked Dad when he came in the house for his afternoon cup of coffee. The potatoes were large and had a smooth, caramel-colored skin, and Dad had raised them in our garden.

"Are you sure," Mom said as she started to peel the potato, "that you can be very careful with the jar? So you don't break it? I wouldn't want anyone to get hurt on the glass."

"Oh, yes. I can be careful with the jar," I said.

"Okay, then. We'll have Dad get some cream tonight when you go out to the barn to do the chores."

"Thanks Mom!" I said.

My mother shook her head. "What kind of a mother would I be if I told you that you couldn't have cream for a school project?"

That evening, when we were ready to put the milkers together, my father brought a quart jar to the milkhouse.

"I'll get the cream now, and then you can take it in the house and put it in the refrigerator. This way, we'll be done with it and neither one of us will forget," he said, as he reached for the shiny aluminum dipper hanging on a nail in the milkhouse. On hot summer days, the dipper came in handy for getting a drink of water. Drinking water from the dipper was a whole lot more fun than going into the house and drinking water out of a glass.

After Dad had skimmed the third dipper of cream, I realized the quart was already half full.

"I only need half..." I said, as he poured more cream into the jar.

Dad looked over at me while the last few drops slid off the edge of the dipper. "As long as I'm skimming cream, I might as well fill it. If somebody else forgets, you'll have a little bit of extra."

I watched as Dad skimmed another dipper of cream. "If someone forgets? No one will forget."

"Well," my father said, "you never know."

A short while later, I took the quart of cream to the house.

"I only needed half, but Dad filled the jar," I said to my mother.

"Good. Then you'll have extra if you need it. You should take an extra jar and an extra cover too."

"That's what Dad said, that I'd have extra cream if I needed it, in case someone else forgets."

"He's right. Someone else might forget," Mom replied.

"No one will forget," I said. "The other kids *promised*."

I had lost count of the number of times my mother had said promises were not to be taken lightly, and if I promised to do something, I must make sure I did what I had promised.

"Just the same," Mom said, "take an extra jar and a cover."

"But the other kids *promised*," I repeated.

"Not everyone does what they say they will do," Mom said.

"But," I said, "you always say that if I promise to do something, I should make sure I do it."

"Yes, and *you're* going to bring the cream you promised you would bring. But not everyone is so careful about keeping promises."

"The other kids will bring cream. You'll see," I said.

"Maybe, maybe not," Mom replied.

Right up until the time I walked into my classroom the next morning, I was convinced that everyone who had promised would bring cream.

As it turned out, I was the only one who remembered.

"I can't believe this," the teacher muttered to herself. "I should have sent a note home. Or called. Or both."

The other kids who were supposed to bring cream stood beside her desk, looking sheepish.

"Dad filled a whole quart," I said, as I set the paper bag on the teacher's desk. "And Mom sent two quart jars."

The teacher's expression brightened. "A whole quart? And *two* jars? Well, I guess we can make our butter after all. We won't end up with as much as I had planned, but half is better than nothing."

"When are we going to make butter?" one of my classmates asked.

"This afternoon," the teacher said.

"What are the crackers and knives for?" someone else wondered.

Several packages of saltine crackers, along with some butter knives, sat on the counter by the window.

"The cooks sent the crackers and knives from the kitchen. That's so we can taste our butter when we are finished," the teacher explained.

Early in the afternoon, we began passing the jars around the room to take turns shaking them. The jars slowly made their way down one aisle and up the next.

"This is fun!" said one girl when she finished her turn at shaking the jar.

"If you say so," said one of the boys.

After the jars had made several circuits, another boy decided enough was enough. "How long is this going to take, anyway?" he asked with an exasperated sigh.

Today the teacher was wearing a bright pink dress with a black patent leather belt and black patent leather shoes to match.

"I don't know how long this is going to take," she said. "We'll just have to keep going until we find out."

So, we continued passing the jars up and down the rows.

At last, one girl let out a shriek. "I see something!" she cried. "I see something!"

The entire class rushed to her desk. Or as close as we could get to her desk. There wasn't room for all of us. But as the jar passed from one hand to the next, sure enough, we could see that bits of yellow had begun to appear in the white cream.

"It's almost finished now," the teacher said.

With renewed energy, we continued passing the jars from one to another, shaking them for all they were worth.

The other jar soon followed with bits of yellow in the white cream.

A little while later, the teacher announced that we were finished with the jars.

"The next step," our teacher explained, "is to strain out the liquid. That's called buttermilk. And then what will be left will be our butter."

After straining the liquid and pressing the small lumps of butter into one big lump and mixing in some salt, the teacher handed out the crackers and knives. We didn't have as much butter as she had planned, but still, there was enough so each of us could taste it. And not only that, but the teacher set aside a small amount so I could take some home for Mom and Dad.

When I arrived home later in the afternoon, my mother was anxious to hear how our experiment had turned out.

"It's been so long since I've had homemade butter, I've forgotten what it's like. Did it taste as good as the butter we get from the milk hauler?" Mom asked.

"Better," I said.

I set the paper bag on the table and pulled out a quart jar. "And guess what? The teacher sent some home for you!"

"Well," Mom said, as she looked at the dab of butter in the bottom of the jar, "wasn't that nice of her."

"Are you going to taste it now?" I asked.

"Let's wait until Dad comes in," Mom said, "and then he can have some too."

I had already put two saltine crackers and a butter knife on the table by the time my father came in from feeding the cows.

"What's that for?" Dad asked.

"The teacher sent some butter home for you and Mom," I said.

I carefully spread a little butter on each cracker and handed one to Mom and one to Dad. Then I watched closely as they bit into their crackers.

"Mmmmmm," Mom said, "this is very good butter."

"It sure is," Dad said. "What did you think of it, kiddo?"

I drew myself up straight and squared my shoulders. "I thought it was the *best* homemade butter I've ever had!"

As my mother looked at me, I could see she was trying not to smile.

"It's the best homemade butter you've ever had because it's the *only* homemade butter you've ever had," she said.

In fact—now that she mentioned it—it *was* the only homemade butter I had ever eaten.

Then again, the cream came from cows I knew personally. And that has to count for something. Doesn't it?

****

~ Appendix A ~

~ How to Make Homemade Ice Cream ~ (Without an Ice Cream Maker!)

Dad's favorite recipe for making ice cream required an ice cream maker. When I was growing up, he would make ice cream several times during the summer, for the Fourth of July, birthdays, when we were going to have a picnic in the backyard, or "just because."

Much to my regret, I never thought to ask Dad to write down his recipe, but if you would like to enjoy the taste of homemade ice cream and don't have the time or the inclination to make it with an ice cream maker, this recipe for ice cream results in a product that is close to the ice cream I enjoyed when I was growing up on our farm.

- 2 eggs
- 3/4 cup sugar
- 2 tablespoons cornstarch
- 1 cup milk
- 1 pint heavy whipping cream
- pinch of salt
- 2 teaspoons vanilla

Using an electric mixer, beat the eggs for several minutes until thick and lemon colored. Add 1 cup of milk and blend into the eggs. Mix sugar and cornstarch in a large saucepan. Add egg/milk mixture to the sugar and cornstarch. Cook until thick (about 5 minutes) stirring constantly. Allow the custard mixture to cool to room temperature.

When the custard is cool, put into a freezer-safe bowl. Blend in cream and salt. Freeze for 2 hours or until slushy. Add 2 teaspoons vanilla.

Whip for 5 to 10 minutes with an electric mixer. Return to freezer and finish freezing (several hours or overnight).

Variations:
After you have whipped the ice cream, fold in 1 to 2 cups of fresh or frozen fruit, nuts and/or chocolate before returning the ice cream to the freezer to finish freezing.

Here are some ideas for additions to your ice cream:
Strawberries
Blackberries
Raspberries
Peaches
Cherries (or Maraschino Cherries)
Chocolate chips
Butterscotch chips
Crushed Heath bars
Crushed peppermint candy
Chopped walnuts
Chopped pistachio nuts
Diced bananas
Coconut
Chocolate chip cookie dough (drop into the ice cream by small spoonfuls and carefully fold in)
Caramel or chocolate or fudge syrup (drop into the ice cream by small spoonfuls and carefully fold in)

****

~ Norma's Homemade Bread ~

My mother used to bake bread about once a week when I was growing up. Store-bought bread, she said, was "too fluffy" and "doesn't taste like anything." Here's the recipe for my mother's bread:

• 4 cups milk
• 1 stick butter (or margarine)
• 1/3 cup sugar
• 2 packages dry yeast (or 4 teaspoons bulk yeast)
• 1 teaspoon salt
• 8 to 10 cups of flour

Measure the milk into a saucepan, add the stick of butter (or margarine) and warm over medium heat until the butter/margarine melts.

Allow the hot milk mixture to cool to lukewarm. Stir in the yeast. Add the sugar and the salt. Add 2 cups of flour and beat until smooth. Add 1 more cup of flour and continue beating until smooth. Stir in the remaining flour. Knead until smooth, 5 to 10 minutes.

Place in a large greased bowl and put in a warm place to rise for one hour. Punch down dough. Shape into loaves and put into greased loaf pans. Place in a warm place to rise for another 45 minutes.

Bake at 350 degrees for 35 minutes or until loaves are light brown and sound hollow when tapped.

Brush the loaves with shortening after you take them out of the oven to keep the crust soft. Let cool 5 or 10 minutes and remove from pans.

Makes 3 large loaves or 4 medium loaves.

****

~ Acknowledgements ~

Thank you to my husband, Randy Simpson, who is fond of saying he is my "biggest fan." His favorite time to say this, by the way, is on hot summer days when he stands in front of me and flaps his arms up and down. "See?" he'll say, "I'm you're biggest fan!"

Randy also is my website designer, my business partner, my administrative assistant, my book cover designer—and an endless source of encouragement.

Additional thanks are due to my brother and sister-in-law, Ingman and Mary Ellen Ralph, and to my sister and brother-in-law, Loretta and Donald Roetter. They represent the small family dairy farmers who 'lived the good life' on their family farms.

And last, but not least, thank you to my readers. I've said it before, and I'll say it again: without readers, writers wouldn't have a job!

****

~ About the Author ~

LeAnn R. Ralph earned an undergraduate degree in English with a writing emphasis from the University of Wisconsin-Whitewater and also earned a Master of Arts in Teaching from UW-Whitewater. She worked as a newspaper reporter for nine years and also has taught English at a boys' boarding school.

The author lives in rural Wisconsin with her husband, two dogs, one horse and assorted cats and is working on her next book, *Cream of the Crop*, another collection of true stories.

If you would like to receive notification when LeAnn's next book is available, write to her at E6689 970th Ave., Colfax, WI 54730, or e-mail her at — bigpines@ruralroute2.com

In addition to *Give Me a Home Where the Dairy Cows Roam*, LeAnn is the author of the books, *Christmas in Dairyland (True Stories from a Wisconsin Farm)* (trade paperback; August 2003; $13.95) and *Preserve Your Family History (A Step-by-Step Guide for Writing Oral Histories)* (e-book; April 2004; $7.95).

****

~ How to Order More Books ~

Here's how to order more copies of *Give Me a Home Where the Dairy Cows Roam* and *Christmas in Dairyland (True Stories from a Wisconsin Farm)*:

• Order on the Internet through Booklocker.com
• Order on the Internet through Amazon.com or Barnes & Noble.
• Order through your local bookstore.
• Call LeAnn at (715) 962-3368.
• Write to LeAnn at E6689 970th Ave.; Colfax, WI 54730
• Order from LeAnn's website—www.ruralroute2.com
    When you order books directly from the author (either by calling, writing or ordering through www.ruralroute2.com), you can request autographed copies with personalized inscriptions. And no need to pre-pay. An invoice will be sent with your order.

****

Remember: Autographed books make great gifts for Christmas, birthdays, graduations, and other special occasions!

****

Read More Books By . . .
LeAnn R. Ralph
(715) 308-6336

~ Preserve Your Family History ~

The e-book includes step-by-step instructions for interviewing friends and family members, along with more than 400 "ready to use" questions on 30 different topics.

To order *Preserve Your Family History (A Step-by-Step Guide for Writing Oral Histories)* (e-book; 65 pages; April 2004; $7.95) visit—www.booklocker.com.

For more information about *Preserve Your Family History*, visit—www.ruralroute2.com.

****

~ A Favor to Ask ~

If you have enjoyed reading *Give Me a Home Where the Dairy Cows Roam* and/or *Christmas in Dairyland (True Stories from a Wisconsin Farm),* would you please do a favor for me?

I would appreciate it if you would recommend my books to family, friends, co-workers or anyone else you think might enjoy them (your child's teacher or your local librarian, for example).

Thank you!

LeAnn R. Ralph
Colfax, Wisconsin

****

CPSIA information can be obtained at www.ICGtesting.com
Printed in the USA
LVOW061347041211

257714LV00001B/8/A